Like fine musical instruments, cats are in perfect harmony with human life. When we understand their motivations, as a musician understands his instrument, we can handle them in much the same way—with full assurance of the rewarding results. By the time you finish this book, your relationship with your cat should be like that between Van Cliburn and his piano.

THE BIGGEST LITTLE CAT BOOK IN THE WORLD

A guide to understanding and caring madly for your cat

Helen Powers

BALLANTINE BOOKS • NEW YORK

Library of Congress Catalog Card Number: 77-79647

ISBN 0-345-36296-9

Manufactured in the United States of America

First Ballantine Books Edition: December 1989

God made the cat in order to give man
the pleasure of petting the tiger.

—ANON

Contents

With thanks and appreciation to Joanne Lockwood, the Housatonic Cat Club, Dianne Lillis and Peep, Morris Animal Foundation, Jack Douglas, Northside Animal Hospital, Nancy Bell at the A.S.P.C.A. in New York City, Rhonda Douglas at *Shelter Sense* magazine, and the Humane Society of the United States in Washington, D.C.

Introduction

Taking a unique approach to the subject of cat ownership, I have attempted to compile a self-help book for cat owners. This is therefore a survival manual rather than a textbook.

The Biggest Little Cat Book in the World is concerned with why cats do what they do, what they're trying to say, their methods of communicating with their owners, and the realistic responses that can be expected from a cat (undivided indifference).

Along with pointers on how to select a cat, I have set out a simple method for recognizing the ancestral history of the cat that might have selected you. Instead of itemizing and explaining the assortment of diseases your cat *might* contract, I have concentrated on the symptoms that signify illness so that the owner can get the necessary diagnosis and professional help when it is needed.

Training and care have been approached from the cat's point of view. Contrary to their reputations, cats are as predictable as any other form of life, and once we understand their psychology, it is not difficult to recognize and avoid the circumstances that will cause them to become hostile or aggressive.

Like fine musical instruments, cats are in perfect harmony with human life. Once we understand their motivations, as a musician understands his instrument, we can handle them in much the same way with full assurance of the rewarding results. By the time you finish this book, your relationship with your cat should be like that between Van Cliburn and his piano.

CHAPTER 1

All Cats Great and Small

If you are already a cat owner, you will not be surprised to learn that your pet is one of the proudest, most prized animals known to mankind. It is also one of the most intelligent, occasionally the most mischievous, and invariably the most mysterious. Once you have scrutinized the history of the domestic cat, you will regard your *Felis catus* with a newfound respect as you come to recognize its awesome ancestry and its refined uniqueness in the animal kingdom.

What's in a Name?

To begin with, every form of life upon this earth is classified. Painstaking research would indicate that the classification of animal life is at best a free-for-all among zoologists, paleontologists, and taxonomists. Since taxonomy is in itself the science of identifying, naming, and classifying all living organisms—after their differences and similarities have been duly assessed by zoologists and paleontologists—it is not difficult to see where disagreement could result.

There is complete accord that cats belong to the order *Carnivora*, which includes all flesh-eating animals, and the family *Felidae*, which is the cat family in general. After that it's anybody's guess. Some scientists believe cats belong to one genus, *Felis*; others list as many as twenty-eight distinct genera.

The most popular method among taxonomists is to classify cats in three genera: *Panthera* (the great cats); *Acinonyx* (the cheetah); and *Felis* (this takes in all the rest, including but not limited to the totally independent ball of fur who is at this moment shedding hair on your living room sofa).

Obviously there are a wide variety of cats who are neither lions, nor tigers, nor cheetahs, and these must be heavily subdivided into species under the genus *Felis*. Your kitty has been a pawn of scientific parley for many years. In 1758 he was officially labeled *Felis catus*, but the category was apparently misfiled by a lovesick clerk and forgotten, because in 1777 along came another scientist who identified the domestic cat as *Felis domestica*. His decision was reinforced officially in 1788 and again in 1829. It was some questionable time after this that the first label, *Felis catus*, showed up under some turkey's lunch box, and according to taxonomical law, the first designation is permanent and irreversible. Therefore the popularity of *Felis domestica* had to give way to the earlier name, *Felis catus*.

In the meantime, however, *Felis catus* had been applied to another member of the genus, the European wildcat, a reasonably close relative of our present-day lap-warmer. Obviously the wildcat of Europe and the domestic cats of the world could not carry the same species identification, so the scientists named the wildcat *Felis sylvestris*. This would appear to settle the matter, but the argument still arises, and there are those in the hierarchy of the cat kingdom who still prefer *Felis domestica* to *Felis catus*.

That your cat has survived all these years of controversy as to who he is, what he is, and where he belongs, is in itself a tribute to his staying power. It may also account for the smug look on his face. He's the only one who knows for sure whether he's a *Felis domestica* or a *Felis catus*, and he's not about to tell.

Once upon a *Miacis*

Kitty probably had his ancestral beginnings with the *miacis*, a bad-mouthed, evil-tempered, weasel-like grouch that roamed the face of prehistoric earth about 50,000,000 years ago. The miacis, unfortunately, was busy with other things, like survival, and maintained no written records of his own existence; so what happened after that is mainly educated conjecture on the part of science, founded upon archaeological discoveries, ancient artwork, evolutionary patterns, and present-day knowledge of genetics. Put together, it makes a decent network of supportive evidence.

It is not known how the unpleasant personality characteristics of the miacis were determined, but possibly archaeologists found fossils of human legs with teethmarks in them. In any event, we shall accept him as a reasonably unpopular beast who would have been socially unacceptable in the club car. Through the milleniums of evolution he fathered not only our friendly domestic kitty cat, but many of our other pets as well, such as the dog, the raccoon, the civet, and the bear. The cat as we know it today first appeared about 10,000,000 years later, which is even longer than it takes a postcard to go from Yuma, Arizona, to Washington, D.C. The cats that existed at that time were not typical parlor Persians, but probably more closely resembled the civet whose anal secretion is one of the most popular fixatives for expensive perfumes. (If this knowledge were made public, it could put Lanvin out of business as it would be back to vanilla extract for all of us. "Promise her anything, but give her civet cat's anal secretion" would never make it in *Vogue*.)

Moving through history, it has been learned that about 4,000 years ago the Egyptians showed the first confirmed affinity for cats as both household pets and deities. Captivated by their quiet grace and

4

beauty, Egyptian craftsmen designed furniture and jewelry in the likeness of cats. Then they went overboard and began worshiping cats as gods. The Egyptian goddess, Bast, who represented the life-giving heat of the sun, was portrayed as having the head of a cat. Anyone who harmed a cat was punished. The penalty for killing a cat was death, so it was unlikely that anyone put the cat out at night—if it didn't come back the next morning, the offender could be held responsible with his life.

Cat owners shaved their eyebrows in mourning when their pets passed on. Some of the Egyptians built stone temples for their cats and buried them in gold coffins. Other dead cats were mummified and laid to heavenly rest in cat cemeteries with mummified mice and rats and little saucers of rapidly souring milk. The cat was at the height of his popularity and power.

Aside from his mysterious beauty, all this honor came to the unctuous cat because he kept rodents away from the buildings and the great storehouses of grain in Egypt. His gift for extermination was quickly recognized by the Africans as well, as they began to lure the African wildcat, or kaffir cat, into their camps with food. As they tamed the animals and kept them about, the tribesmen were impressed by the improved sanitary conditions in the sudden absence of mice and rats. Putting two and two together, they concluded that there was a strong connection between the presence of the cats and the elimination of the rats.

It was probably for the same reasons that the

Phoenician traders carried Egyptians cats on their ships to Europe. Here they cross-bred with various bad-tempered European wildcats to produce the first domestic cats of Europe. Again they were given high community standing because of their ability to kill rodents, especially during the Black Plague of the eleventh century.

During the Middle Ages their reputations were tarnished when they again became objects of worship—this time by conjurors and sorcerors. They were viewed as objects of evil spirits associated with devils and witchcraft. The cat population diminished to a certain extent. Even today they are portrayed as the familiars of mystics. Things balanced out by the 1700s, when the Europeans brought their cats to the New World and they became the ancestors of most of the cats in the United States today.

If You Can't Find a Cat, a Wombat Will Do

It is generally believed that cats had been distributed throughout the world since prehistoric times with the exception of Australia, its satellite islands, and Madagascar. This omission is not totally explained by science, but it is probable that these islands were cut off from the main land masses at a time prior to the development and distribution of cats in other parts of the world. No placental mammals are indigenous to Australia. There were, however, animals in Australia called native cats or tiger cats which didn't look or act like cats, and were, in fact, not cats at all but native marsupials related to the kangaroo and the wombat. No one knows why the Australians called these creatures cats, but possibly since there were no cats in Australia, they didn't know what they were supposed to be like. Since they lived in one of the few places in the world without cats, and didn't want to feel slighted, they created their own—from kangaroos. It is interesting that the word *cat*, or something very similar to it, is almost universal as the name for this favored household pet.

The *Dinictus* and *Hoplophoneus* (Who Cares?)

Early cats were divided into two groups, *Dinictus* and *Hoplophoneus*. The *Hoplophoneus* had exaggerated upper canine teeth that wouldn't fit in his mouth without orthodontia, so he was equipped with a flange on his lower jaw to protect them. The saber-toothed tiger was a species of *Hoplophoneus*, designated *Smilodon* by a paleontologist with a sense of humor. "Smiley" was a formidable enemy and a fierce fighter. He could open his jaws very wide and snap them shut with fantastic force supported by the strength of his powerful neck and the weight of his massive body. However, swift he was not. As the slower forms of life that he existed on died out, so did Smiley. He was too clumsy to overtake the more agile animals and became extinct.

Modern cats come from the group *Dinictus*. Beautifully suited to competitive existence and survival, they were fast moving, adaptable, intelligent, and equipped by nature to prosper. With minor exceptions, they remain unchanged to this day.

Panthera

Examining our cat's relatives in order to better understand his nature, we look first at the genus *Panthera*. This includes the lions, tigers, leopards, and jaguars, or the "big cats" as they are called in the circus. Because they are anatomically identical lions and tigers, it should be noted, can interbreed (with a little help from a curious zookeeper). Since there are no tigers in Africa, and hardly any lions any place else in the world, the only opportunity they have to crossbreed is in captivity. When this happens they produce cubs called tiglons or ligers, the first half of the name indicating the gender of the sire. The male always gets top billing.

Without their distinctive skins, as mentioned before, lions and tigers are the same animals. But here's the catch: these cats have strikingly different personalities. The lion is a lovable coward. He is easily frightened by anything from an explorer's drip-dry laundry fluttering in the breeze, to little children running toward his cage. A pride of lions will consist of five or six male and female animals. They kill to eat when hungry. The lions drive the prey to the lionesses who must perform the killing and prepare the meal. The lion then shows up to eat it. As long as they are well fed, they are harmless, as they are not "man-eaters." Lions and tigers eat people only when they can't get anything better.

Tigers, on the other hand, are fierce and aggressive. More powerful than lions, they kill not only for food but for blood lust as well. They are bold and fearless. In India entire villages have been evacuated when a man-eating tiger was on the prowl. However, the man-eaters are not the strong, young tigers, as one might expect, but the older ones whose teeth are worn down and whose energy is diminished. They find it easier to stalk and kill a human than another animal, and so turn to this manner of subsistence.

Tigers are usually orange and black striped, not unlike some of our household cats, but they also come in white. These are rare albino strains. Leopards are spotted and there are no albinos. However, they have a tendency toward melanism (black mutation), and when this occurs, they are called panthers. A panther is actually a black leopard. The term *panther* is a misnomer, as it refers to the genus *Panthen* which properly describes any great cat that roars.

Leopards are far deadlier than lions or tigers. They frequently develop a taste for human flesh and become man-eaters. They will kill anything that moves. The large *Panthera* are not arboreal, but the leopard, being smaller than either lions or tigers, is a tree climber. From an outstretched branch he will spring on his prey and kill it. He is also very intelligent and rather tricky. Leopards have been reported to fake seizures on the ground in order to attract the attention of a herd of antelope, then jump up and have them for dinner.

The only great cats in America are the ferocious jaguars. They are found in Arizona and New Mexico, although a portly gentleman with a white mustache was sighted driving one recently on the New Jersey Turnpike. These spotted tree climbers may be albino or melanist. They do not eat humans, but can digest nearly anything else. They love to swim, and once in the water will even tackle alligators.

So much for the great cats, but at one time or another, you have no doubt seen part of each of them in your own little tabby, whose complex personality is a splendid combination of all of them.

Meet-a-Cheetah

The only species in the genus *Acinonyx* is the cheetah, which is anatomically different from all the other cats. The cheetah is reportedly a tractable, large cat that makes an excellent pet and can be easily trained. Since ancient times, they have been used as hunters and retrievers in Asia and Egypt. They have been clocked at 60 m.p.h. and are believed to be able to do 75 m.p.h. on a fast track. The cheetah's claws are blunt and not totally retractable. With the exception of certain parts of Africa the cheetah is virtually extinct.

Felis Catus

The genus *Felis* includes our own *catus*, along with the puma, ocelot, margay, serval, lynx, and bobcat.

The puma (cougar or mountain lion) is the second largest cat in America (the jaguar is the first), and the most misunderstood. Ranchers have claimed that cougars kill their livestock, but the cougars deny this, insisting they only destroy pests that need to be controlled. With hindquarters higher than head and chest, a mountain lion can spring twenty feet in one jump. The serval looks like a dog with a cat's head. The lynx also has longer hind legs, stub tail, broad paws, tufted ears, and muttonchop whiskers. With sly intelligence, he will walk in another animal's tracks for great distances to mislead a pursuer.

The bobcat is a variety of lynx. He is also called a wildcat. Arboreal, he climbs trees and springs like a panther. Wildcats often mate with domestic cats, and their bobtailed babies hop like bunnies. Farm cats frequently seem to show signs of this wildness.

Also in the lynx family are the jungle cats. However, they are never found in jungles. They prefer open, hot, dry scrubland called *jangal* in Hindustani, from which the word *jungle* is derived. Smaller than the lynx, but larger than domestic cats, they have wistful, haunting facial expressions which can be deceiving. These, too, interbreed freely with domestic cats.

Add to all these the beautiful ocelots and margays, both of which can be tamed and maintained as exotic pets, and you have a reasonably clear picture of the cat kingdom of which your pet is a part. Curled up on the hearth, he is a member of the family. Once outside the house, however, he reverts to the primitive instincts of his progenitors, stalking and springing, attacking and defending, moaning and howling like a stranger. But the minute he crosses the threshold of home, he sheds the role of jungle beast. Wrapping himself in an aura of innocence, he plays the part of pussycat again. He is as complex as the ages have made him.

CHAPTER 2

Selecting Your Feline Pet, or Why a Free Cat Is a Great Buy

The addition of any pet to a household should be a carefully considered matter. Whether you live in a sprawling villa or a one-room efficiency, there are a lot of good reasons why a cat makes an ideal pet.

Cats are quiet. They need very little space, a minimum of care, and they're clean. It is also cheaper to feed a cat than a St. Bernard. They are devoted, affectionate, and understanding. You can tell your cat anything and he'll still love you. If you lose your job or your best friend, your cat will think no less of you. Your cat will never threaten your popularity by barking at three in the morning. He won't attack the mailman or eat the drapes, although he may climb the drapes to see how the room looks from the ceiling. (He's very curious.)

13

He might occasionally manicure his nails on your Chippendale sofa, or devour a bowl of shrimp left on a counter ten minutes before guests arrive. However, this is usually the extent of his mischievousness.

Once you have decided to become a cat owner, there are other decisions you will have to make. You will want to decide on sex, breed, age, and where you will find the fulfillment of your feline dreams at a price you can afford to pay, but let's digress and explore the prospect of compatibility between you and your kitty.

Pussycat Psychology

People who are put off by cats don't understand them. A cat's behavior is just as predictable as a dog's. If he doesn't like having his stomach touched (many cats don't), but you persist in doing it, he will scratch you. If you pick him up when he's in a state of fright or panic, he may misinterpret his rescue as an entrapment and claw his way free. A cat does not display hostility unless he feels his rights are being violated.

A very young kitten may attempt to cling to your ankle as you walk across a room or spring at you unexpectedly from a hidden lair. He plays with everything that moves, and your leg is just as appealing as a toy mouse. However, by the time he's seven or eight months old, he can be trusted not to scratch any member of his family, provided the family does its part and respects the rule of tolerance which he has assertively established. He develops cunning and magnificent nonaggressive defenses. If he doesn't want to ride in your child's doll buggy, he's not going to tear off her arm. He's an excellent escape artist and will take the first opportunity to get his agile body out of the buggy and up the nearest tree. It is unfair to describe cats as treacherous. They can be trusted and anticipated more often than people.

While there may be isolated cases of cats that are genetically "bad," usually they are the most adaptable of animals. When you walk through the door with a pick of the litter, your new kitten will readily adjust to your family situation, including your full-grown Doberman pinscher (who will quickly learn to stand off from this awesome three pound terror), an exuberant eighteen-month toddler, and a near-sighted grandparent who keeps stepping on him. Cats are tolerant and compatible.

With regard to cats and children, the well-adjusted two-year-old, when presented a kitten, will respond with loving, gentle care that comes from an instinctive desire to protect this helpless, smaller creature. A child learns this from his environment and his parents. If, on the other hand, a child exhibits cruel or vicious behavior, it is quite predictable that he will demonstrate little reverence or respect for a kitten's vulnerability and he should not have one. Normally the parenting instinct prevails, and your child will not need supervised instructions on treatment of a cat. Every time he strokes his kitty, his behavior will be reinforced when this love is instantly returned. A mutual understanding will quickly grow between them.

An infant and a kitten are less compatible. However, a mature cat will welcome the new addition to the family and all the warm blankets that accompany it. For this reason, it is unwise to allow the family cat to be alone in the baby's room. He will take great joy in sleeping in the crib close to this warm, new life. The problem this presents is not that the cat will suck the baby's breath and suffocate him (an old wives' tale that grew from misunderstanding) but that in a moment of intense love, the cat will decide to sleep on the top of the baby, a burden the infant's fragile body is not ready to accept. When the baby is with other members of the family, the cat can be trained not to jump into the playpen or onto your lap when you are holding or feeding the infant. Cats respond well to mild reprimands and quickly learn right from wrong.

Considering the small margin of physical difference between cats, their individuality is overwhelming. They are great imitators, and will assume the characteristics of their environments. In a mixed household of dogs, cats, children, and adults, they will absorb something from each of these. One of our cats learned from our dogs to scratch on the door when he wanted in or out. Another one of the cats has established a connection between the opening of a door and the door knob, so when he wants in or out, he stands on his hind legs and stretches his long, lithe body until he can reach the knob and

rattle it. The next thing he will want is a key. I have
heard of cats that can turn on a light switch if they
are alone after dark, or can ring the doorbell when
they want to come in. In inclement weather, we
have a cat who will go into the bathroom, close the
door, and, somewhat to our distress, utilize the con-
veniences of modern plumbing for his personal relief.

When we brought a five-week-old Doberman
pinscher into our house with two adult cats, she was
delighted to find reasonable replacements for the
playful siblings she had left behind. She didn't know
what cats were—she had never seen one. In the
first few weeks that she was with us, they were her
behavior models. We would see the Dobie sitting up
on her haunches, batting at the cats with her paws.
In the domestic animal kingdom it is usually the
smallest of these who calls the shots. The cats laid
down the law to the Doberman, who wouldn't
dream of defying them, but when a two-month-old
miniature poodle joined the group around the
hearth, it was the poodle who became head honcho.
She regulated the traffic flow and told the animals
where they could go and at what speed. She will not
allow the Siamese to scratch the furniture; she fero-
ciously guards trash waiting at the back door, she
polices every room in the house. The Doberman
could wipe her out with one paw, and the cats could
remove her face with their claws, but no one ques-
tions her authority or resists it. She makes the other
animals so nervous when she pounces on them, or

curls her lip and yelps, that they would rather avoid her than tangle with her. In any event, some natural hierarchy is observed and honored, and it may be worth keeping in mind if you have one pet and are considering another. After a few days of monitoring, you will have established order, and they will work out leadership for themselves.

In most instances where a cat has a warped personality or a wildness that cannot be controlled, there is usually a reason, and more likely than not the reason is that the cat is left alone for long periods of time. Many cats, in fact most of them, seem to adjust to this situation as they do to everything else, but it does seem to be the Achilles' heel in the cat psyche. They like companionship, or the presence of someone else in the house. The less they are left alone, the more gentle and docile they become. This is why two cats are better than one.

Within your cat's highly developed personality are exceptional communicative skills. As your rapport develops, your cat will tell you what he wants. If you are in one room, and what he wants is in another, he will meow to get your attention and then lead you to it. He may take you to the refrigerator or the front door. He will make his needs quite clear. As your communication becomes more refined, the sound of his meow will tell you what he wants before he shows you.

His body language speaks for itself. If you hold your cat against his will, or in an uncomfortable position, his tail will begin to twitch—his way of warning you of his discontent. When King Kitty walks through the room with his tail up over his back and the tip turned under, he is pleased with himself and the world at large. When he is about to do combat with another animal, his ferocity will be expressed through guttural hissing and an arched back. His fear at this moment is signified by a bushy tail. It is not unusual to let your cat in from the outdoors and notice that his tail is twice its normal size. He has just had a good scare. In a minute or two the hairs will go down, starting at the body and working out.

Cats are highly intelligent. If they seem less responsive than dogs, it is their show of independence that sometimes deters immediate cooperation. It is impossible to consistently call a cat to your side. He will come if he feels like it. If his mood coincides with yours, he will be happy to respond. When you stand at the door calling "Here, kitty, kitty, kitty," he will answer if he is ready to come in. If not, forget it. A cat will contemplate a situation before plunging into it. He will carefully analyze a height or width before attempting to achieve it. Before going outside, he will pause at the door (unless he's desperate) to make sure there are no things that go bump in the night. The heat loss that his caution creates in mid-winter is minimal, but his analytical nature cannot be rushed. In more frustrating circumstances you can stand with the door open, breathlessly awaiting his next move. If, however, his survey detects foul weather, disagreeably low temperatures, or an unseen animal, he backs off completely.

Some people say cats have a sense of humor, but I've never heard one laugh. With the egocentricity of superstars, they are more concerned with their own image of dignity and beauty than reeling off one-liners like stand-up comics. Because of their high intelligence, cats can be trained to do tricks. However, a cat will not do anything that might make him look like a fool. They never get too old to play, but if the game gets silly, they'll stop.

Unlike dogs who find certain musical tones offensive, cats are music lovers. They will walk across the keys of a piano and create their own music, or if they are genuine groupies, they will hang out near the piano when someone is playing and purr contentedly as they listen. Cats make a wonderful audience.

These are the things you can expect from your cat. He will expect very little from you in return. Outside of the normal care that his dependence requires, he wants the sound of your voice, a little attention (at his discretion, please), and the warmth of your presence.

Twofers

For purposes of companionship, two cats are generally better than one. One pet invariably calls for another. They like to be with their own kind. However, a cat and a dog can become equally as companionable, but cats and birds do not mix well.

With one or two animals already in residence, it is not difficult to introduce a new pet into the circle.

When you bring a new cat into the house, its present animal occupants will realize instinctively that this is not an intruder, so it is important that they be introduced inside rather than out in the yard where any trespasser is an enemy for life. Even mature pets will adapt to each other, or at least reach a reasonable truce. The length of the introductory period depends on the circumstances.

After a company transfer we were living in a hotel with two small children, and a Siamese cat in mid-winter awaiting the arrival of our furniture. Walking a four-year-old up and down the halls one night to exhaust him, we met a man who invited us to come see what he had in his room. He guaranteed we would love it. More curious than cautious, I dragged my son with me back to the man's room, whereupon I told him whatever it was he wanted to show us, we would wait in the hall, and he could bring it out. He did. It was a beautiful black Persian cat, probably about nine or ten months old. The stranger offered it as a gift to my son who responded with wide-eyed acceptance. The man turned out to be a minor celebrity, and told us that the cat had been on the Jack Paar show with him during a recent appearance. Being a sucker for celebrities, I carried the cat back to our room. My husband alluded vaguely to the possibility of a divorce, but the cat stayed. There was no time for formalities. I dropped him on the floor, showed him where the food bowl was, and the two cats never so much as snarled at each other. However, the next day our Old English sheep dog arrived at the airport. When my husband came through the door with her, the new member of the menagerie made one flying leap at the dog's face, and clung tenaciously to her hairy head while the dog ran around greeting each of us, totally unaware that she had a cat hanging from her fur. The cat finally loosened her grip, and everyone had a good night's sleep. Three days later our furniture arrived just as the hotel had begun eviction proceedings.

Subsequently we brought home two small kittens from a nearby farm. They were from the same litter, but obviously the progeny of different sires. One was a solid gray short-haired cat, and the other was a long-haired orange. They were only seven weeks old at the time, and fit into the palm of our hand. The Doberman and the poodle were on hand to welcome them. We put the tiny kittens into a box in the den where we could keep an eye on things, and both dogs thought they were the mother. They shoved and competed, each one wanting to hover over the box and take care of the "babies." The cats ruled the roost until those dogs were gone, and we brought in a new poodle. She arrived as a puppy, much smaller than the big cats, and for some reason, no matter what she did, they never raised a claw at her. The poodle became a tyrant and they were her slaves, but the bonding is remarkable. The three of them sleep curled up together in a pile; the poodle snuggles up to one of the cats and begs to be washed and groomed whereupon the cat lies there licking the poodle's head and ears with her emery tongue; when the poodle comes back from the kennel, the first thing she does is run in to say hello to the cats. They are inseparable.

The hierarchy of nature will be observed and honored, and it may be worth keeping in mind if you have one pet and are considering another. After a few days of monitoring, you will have established order, and the pets will work out leadership for themselves.

Kitten or Adult

The first thing to decide is whether you want a playful kitten or a mature cat. The full-grown cat will earn his keep and be less trouble. This means, however, that you will have to live with this cat's preestablished habits. If his previous owner has been cooking kidneys for him every night, he will not take kindly to commercially prepared cat foods. If he has been accustomed to sleeping on someone's furniture in the past, he's not going to stay off yours. Behavior modification is a slow process.

It would be wise to ask the previous owner about the cat's present diet, his likes and dislikes, his lifestyle, and his idiosyncrasies, if any. In this way you can ease the trauma of transfer by maintaining his established regimen as closely as possible. This will make the adjustment easier for both of you.

A kitten is ready to leave its mother by the time it's two months old. The kitten will adjust more easily to his new home and family, and will quickly adopt the rules of the house. Therefore, the manner in which you start him is the manner in which he will grow. If you soothe his palate with gourmet meals, you'll be cooking them for the rest of his life. Commercially prepared foods come in a wide variety and are both nutritious and tasty, but after a couple of weeks of chopped liver and kidneys, all the Morrises on Madison Avenue won't be able to do a number on him.

Similarly, all other training must take place as soon as he arrives. Once he learns where it is permissible to make his bathroom, whether it be a kitty box or the great outdoors, he will abide by it. He can be trained not to claw the furniture, but if not stopped the minute he starts, your treasured antiques will be ready for recycling. Not all cats are furniture scratchers, but the offenders are irreversibly destructive. I know—I have one.

How to Tell One from the Other

Assuming that you are not a breeder and your cat is to be a family pet, before it is a year old you would be wise to have it "fixed." Having your cat fixed is not the same thing as having your car repaired. Fixing, also known as altering, neutering, or spaying, is a simple sterilization process, and once accomplished the animal's original gender is not that important. Their personalities no longer seem to be as diverse as those of a complete male or female.

How do you tell one from the other? Granted, the differences in a small kitten are subtle, and unless you are getting your kitten from an experienced breeder, it is very difficult to determine the sex of this small animal. More than one person has made an appointment to have their male cat neutered only to discover at the vet's that it needed to be spayed instead.

However, if you want to be certain, here's what you can do. The male sex organs will look like two dots or a colon (:) beneath its tail, while the female will resemble an inverted exclamation point (¡). Whether you get a male or female, once it is fixed it will return the same kind of love and adapt equally well to you and your family.

If your new cat is not fixed, it will be very simple to determine whether it is a male or female. If it is a (¡), it will have kittens. If it is a (:), it will spray on your drapes and furniture when its sex urges are frustrated. Both these pitfalls can be avoided by heeding the professional advice of your veterinarian.

Breeding is best left to breeders. In seven years one female cat and her kittens can produce 420,000 cats. For this reason sterilization is recommended by veterinarians and all animal welfare organizations. Too frequently exuberant parents acquire a female kitten so they can show their three-year-old the process of reproduction. There are 2,000,000 more cats than dogs in the United States, and both species have an overpopulation. It seems unfair to produce another litter of either as a science lesson. In Manhattan alone in 1987, 85,000 dogs and cats were taken in by the A.S.P.C.A. Seventeen thousand were adopted or claimed by their owners, but 60,000 had to be put to sleep.

Pedigree or Paperless Pauper

The next decision is whether you want a registered or unregistered cat. Unless you are a breeder, or looking for a show cat, the registration is a matter of status and price. Unlike pedigreed dogs, each of which is registered with the American Kennel Club, there are a constantly changing number of studbook organizations for cats in the United States, each with varying specifications for the ultimate in a variety of breeds. The largest and oldest of these is the Cat Fanciers' Association, an offshoot of the first cat show in the United States held at the old Madison Square Garden in 1895. In 1909 they compiled their first studbook. The American Cat Association is popular in the Midwest and West, and the Cat Fanciers' Federation is active in the East. If you buy a registered cat, you are paying for, and are entitled to, a certificate of registration attesting to the fact that the cat's records and pedigree are recorded with one or more of the recognized cat associations. The transfer of these papers should be made at the time you pay for the cat.

Breeders will charge 50–100 percent more for a pedigree cat than will a pet shop. This is because breeders keep the best of the litter for private sale. The kittens that do not offer outstanding potential as show material are sold to pet shops for less than half the price you will pay for them there.

If you want a registered cat of a particular breed you can probably find it at a cat show, along with owners who raise and sell them. If show attendance is out of the question, a local veterinarian will be able to give you the names of catteries in your area. You can also find occasional ads for registered cats in your newspaper, or in abundance in *Cats Magazine*.

If you can be happy with an unregistered cat, they are less expensive. Specialized, paperless breeds are advertised in local newspapers at reasonable prices. Assorted cat varieties will be "free to a good home," or available from your local animal shelter for a small donation. While most of these animals will be of questionable origin, they will make marvelous pets. The wide range of unusual choice will include every possible color combination in either a short-haired or long-haired cat.

A Healthy Cat

A healthy cat or kitten will display the same physical characteristics as a healthy person. He will have clear eyes, a thick shiny coat without sign of rash or patches of missing fur, and he will be lively and alert.

Signs that indicate health problems are runny

eyes or nose, sneezing, and ear mites, which are rather difficult to detect. When selecting a kitten, sometimes the least desirable can be the most appealing. A kindle of kittens should be a flurry of nonstop activity. The shy kitten who sits on the sidelines arouses our compassion for losers, but this kitten could be a troublesome and sickly pet. In other words, don't let your heart rule your head.

No matter where you get your kitten or cat, it is a good idea to note his environment and the general condition of other animals on the premises. A fresh-smelling, clean room usually indicates healthy cats. Before you depart with your newfound friend, it is important to determine what shots and inoculations it has had. It should be clearly understood with the owner that you are taking the kitten subject to a complete examination by your vet. Failing to pass this examination, the kitten should be returned, particularly if there are other animals or children in your home. Buying your kitten from a professional breeder would usually assure a clean bill of health. However, if you buy a kitten at a cat show (and they are sometimes on sale at these affairs), it is further reassurance to know that every cat on the premises had to undergo an examination by a veterinarian—so you stand to benefit from this.

Nevertheless, any pet that is brought into the home, whether it wandered to your door or was purposely gotten from a breeder, an agency, or a cat show, should be examined by your vet for less evident problems. This is even more imperative in cases where environmental control was impossible (*i.e.*, a stray who might have been anywhere, or a cat that comes from crowded living quarters where he was in contact with many other animals), and where there are other animals in the house. In addition to checking your cat, the vet will also begin or continue the cat's inoculations against such fatal diseases as distemper and rabies.

On the Other Hand

All previous considerations aside, let's face facts: cats usually select *us*. One day you open the door and there he is. He introduces himself by rubbing against your legs with his motor running, then looks at you with a pleading face that wants nothing more than your love (and does he know how to get it). It's all over for you from that point. Welcome home, kitty!

CHAPTER 3

How to Identify the Cat That Has Selected You

Cat lovers are made, not born. They are converts, and the cats are the missionaries. Cat haters become cat lovers the moment a cat enters their lives. I was a cat hater. I loved dogs until one Mother's Day when my three-year-old son (with a little help from his father) gifted me with a two-month-old Siamese. Since I had been hoping for a Gucci handbag, I was less than thrilled when they walked in the door, but within ten minutes that tiny kitten had completely captivated me. It can happen to anyone.

Since this book is for cat lovers rather than cat breeders, and for cat owners rather than cat fanciers, we shall assume that you are among the vast majority of cat people who simply "come by" their

cats through the normal course of living. In most
instances, we don't consider acquiring a cat—a cat
acquires us. So instead of describing the large variety of breeds that are available for your selection,
we'll try to help you identify the kind of cat you
have acquired through chance. The cart is now pulling the horse.

The first thing that influenced your decision was
availability. The cat was there and so were you. If
you personally selected one over another or from a
group of several, your reasons were the best in the
world. You liked the way it looked. There was
something about the blend of this particular cat's
coloring and eyes, or the way it was marked, that
appealed to you. There is no better or safer way to
choose a cat. Your heart knows, but don't lose your
head if the cat of your choice shows any indications
of poor health.

Chances are your household pet did not come
with a pedigree. Not to worry—every cat is something. The following pages will tell you what to
say when people ask you what kind of cat you
have. Because of the innate dignity of this animal,
he deserves to be called something better than a
stray or an alley cat. No matter how confusing his
lineage may be, he will emerge with definite characteristics that automatically give him a label.
There is no such thing as "just plain old cat." As
dogs crossbreed they tend to lose their identity,
but cats invariably retain a recognizable part of
theirs. If your cat is not a clean-cut model of a

pedigree standard, he will still exhibit the influences of his dominant genes.

Of all the breeds that are recognized by the cat fanciers' associations in the United States, only a few are so completely different in appearance that they can be separated on sight. For the most part the differences are subtle and even the breeders do not always agree. Certainly these minute differences are of no consequence whatsoever to the average cat lover. The relationship between you and your cat is such that if he does not have tufts of fur between his toes, or if his black body had three white hairs, he'll still get tuna dinner.

There are many stories about the origins of certain breeds of cats, most of them interwoven with tales about Eastern royalty, or a soft life in a sultan's palace, but since they are undocumented, they are all questionable. No one knows for sure where the natural breeds came from, or how they began.

Breed names seldom describe with any accuracy the geographical point of origin of a particular cat. Most of the stunning "thoroghbreds" seen at cat shows are man-made through genetic breeding. A purebred dog is a purebred dog, but a purebred cat may be developed from a variety of strains. The main difference between your cat and a pedigree is that no one kept track of his ancestry, making it impossible to duplicate his strain. Purebreds are the product of controlled crossbreeding.

New varieties and breeds are constantly being created by professional breeders skilled in Mendelian genetics. When a pair of cats of two different varieties are bred, the breeder will know almost unfailingly the number, sex, coloring, and type of the resultant kittens before they are born. Certain breeds and types are reproduced through natural genetics; others are artificially created through skillful outbreeding or crossbreeding. Thus it is possible to get a Lynx Point Siamese, or a Himalayan, which is a longhair with Siamese markings. It is also through outbreeding and selective breeding that flaws in the ideal cat's standard are corrected, such as kinks in the tail or crossed eyes.

Since it is quite possible you know nothing about your cat's genealogy, he is the progeny of chance, which sounds much better than calling him a stray or an alley cat. Whether or not he has papers won't affect his beauty, his dignity, or his loving nature. With no knowledge of your cat's heretofore indescribable ancestry, he can be described by identifying his characteristics in three categories:

1. Hair type
2. Color
3. Pattern

Chances are you already know what kind of hair your cat has (either long, short, or curly) since this is not difficult to determine. We'll discuss the long-hairs first.

Longhairs

Angoras were the first long-haired cats on the European continent, appearing about three hundred years ago. The Persian was introduced later. Most of our long-haired cats today which we refer to as Persians are a cross between the Turkish Angoras and the long-haired wildcats of Europe. Generations of cross-breeding and outbreeding virtually wiped out the original Angoras which came from Turkey. The breed has been reestablished, but in white only. The body types of the two long-haired cats are different, and an Angora with a cobby (squat), Persian-type body is disqualified as show material.

Persians are believed to be descended from cats which are still wild in southern regions of the Caspian Sea near the Caucasus. They were brought back to Europe by the Crusaders returning from the Near East where it is said these cats lived in sultans' palaces. Long-haired cats cling to their royal ancestry and never let you forget who they are.

Whether your cat is a Persian or a cross between a Persian and almost anything except a dog, it is quite adequate and very dignified to describe him simply as a longhair. The Persian type has a stocky body on short legs with a silky, luxurious coat. The long-haired cats are gentle and loving with big round eyes and beautiful faces. They come in vast arrays of color and design, and look like small whimsical lions. The tail or "brush" is thick with fur and gives the cat an aura of haughty pride. One of the more distinctive of the long-haired breeds is the Peke-Faced Red which was developed from a red tabby and red self. It has a face like a Pekinese with a wrinkled muzzle and a snub nose that is depressed or indented.

Although the longhairs possess an overwhelming dignity and allure, the nature of their physical structure usually renders them less agile than the short-haired foreign cats. It is not unusual for a long-haired cat to set his sights on a tabletop, crouch for the daring leap, spring, and fall back in disgust when he misses his mark by a foot or so. Aiming at a sunny windowsill, they are quite apt to plow headfirst into a wall. Sensitive to the absurdity of their situation, they seldom make a second attempt until they have reorganized their forces and reappraised the situation. They hate to look silly.

Another glamorous breed is the Chinchilla, a soft, silky, white or silver-ticked cat with large expressive emerald or blue-green eyes. Chinchillas rarely have to catch mice for survival; they are very much in demand for television commercials. Their residuals alone keep them in mackerel.

The Maine Coon Cat is another variety of long-haired cat, found mostly in Maine. Less cobby than the conventional Persian, their bodies are more slender like the Angora. They come in self colors (which are solid shades of one particular color) or tabby markings. Like the Down-Easterners with whom they live, they are tough and hardy. One of the personality characteristics that differentiates the Maine Coon Cat from others is his love for high places. He's apt to choose a high shelf or barn rafters for sleeping. The Maine Coon Cat is in no way related to the raccoon for whom he has been named—they just share a love of climbing.

This group of long-haired cats look more or less alike to the untrained eye, but there is one that is immediately recognizable and distinctive. This is the Himalayan, a new man-made breed first recognized by cat fanciers in 1957. This cat has blue eyes and the color markings of a Siamese, but the build and long-haired coat of a Persian. You might say a Himalayan is a shaggy Siamese. These are beautiful cats which seem to present the best of both worlds. They offer the gentle, loving dispositions of long-hairs with the unusual coloring of the Siamese. However, they are without the demanding nature of the Siamese.

Closely related to the Himalayan in appearance is the Birman. The Birman has the Siamese coat pattern with long hair, but its paws are white, giving it the appearance of wearing gloves.

Shorthairs

Short-haired cats come in two basic models, *domestic* and *foreign*. These words describe their body types rather than their origins. Most of our household cats carry both bloodlines. So do unregistered long-haired cats, which may be part Persian or part fuzzy caterpillar provided the long-hair gene is dominant. Short-haired household cats are rarely undiluted domestics, but may be a modified blend of several things.

The pedigreed Domestic Shorthair is not as common as we might think. He has a chunky body with a very round head, round eyes, and a short neck. He is strong, sturdy, and powerful. Pedigreed Domestic Shorthairs have been bred for ideal markings and type. The pussycat that came to your door in a snowstorm may not be this perfect, but he certainly has identifiable indications of his genetic strain.

The foreign body type is long and slim, very much like the tiger. He has slender legs and may have a heartshaped face with widely spread, sometimes slanted eyes. His ears are usually more pointed than those of the Domestic, and while he will have a delicate, fragile appearance, he, too, is sturdy and strong.

Siamese

The Siamese is the most popular cat in the king-dom today. He is a foreign cat, lean and graceful, with slim legs, oval feet, and a long tail. Contrary to his name, he is not common in Siam; in fact, in that country he is known as the Chinese Cat, probably because of his slanted eyes. He is immediately rec-ognizable not only by his sleek body build, but by his unusual and distinctive markings—dark shad-ings on the muzzle, ears, tail, and feet, called points. Natural genetics have produced the Seal Point, Blue Point, Chocolate Point, Lilac or Laven-der Point. Breeders have artificially produced the Tabby Point (or Lynx Point), by crossing the Sia-mese with the Tabby, Red Point, Tortie Point, and Cream Point. The bodies of these cats are light-col-ored, ranging from almost white to the creamy beige of the Seal Point, with points of beautifully shaded brown, blue or lavender. Their almond-shaped eyes are bright blue and occasionally crossed. The adult color of a Siamese may be diffi-cult to determine since they are solid white at birth and the points may not show up for a couple of months. If you are contemplating a Siamese kitten, or want to establish the color points that the adult cat will have, this can be determined by looking at the pads on the bottom of its paws. The Chocolate Point will have pale brown pads, the Blue Point will

38

have gray pads, and the Lilac Point will have frosty gray or pink pads.

Anything any other cat has, the Siamese will have more of. They deal in excess. They are more intelligent, more curious, more sensitive, and more loving. They are also greedier, sexier, noisier, and more demanding than other cats. They are gregarious, mischievous, and entertaining. In essence, they are "cattier" than other cats.

The Siamese craves companionship. For this reason they are frequently owned in pairs. They are extremely social and don't relish long hours alone. They are more extroverted than other cats. If you try to take a nap, your Siamese will jump on your stomach, walk up your body, and drape himself around your neck. You don't own him—he owns you. If you are sitting in a chair reading the newspaper, he'll leap onto your lap and you'll find your nose buried in print. If he can't be on top of you, he'll find the softest, warmest thing in the house—an afghan, a mink coat, or a basket of laundry—and sleep on that.

Because of his great love for warmth and comfort the Siamese will map out the "sunshine route" in the house where he lives. He knows just where the sun will be and when, and he will follow it around all day. There will be little variation in his route.

The Siamese has longer hind legs than front legs and is an agile jumper. They are fond of high places. Ours eats on top of the refrigerator. We began putting his food bowl there when not in use so the Doberman wouldn't wipe it out. The Siamese didn't question this unusual custom and began jumping up there to eat. Every evening when we have dinner, he sits on top of a cabinet nearby and watches us.

A Siamese can't resist an open door and is liable to be closed into closets, cabinets, and boxes. He will sleep in a drawer if one is open. They are curious, but agile cats. More than once, mine has jumped into my dollhouse and moved his graceful body about, peeking into rooms without knocking over a single piece of tiny furniture.

Most cats dislike noise, and the Siamese is extremely put off by it. Mine will hide if he sees a vacuum cleaner. He runs from a roll of foil the minute it is removed from the shelf. Siamese generally loathe sanitation trucks. Our cat's predecessor once jumped over my head as I was standing in the doorway when the garbageman came. What he didn't anticipate was that the door behind me leading to the basement would be open, so he kept right on going. It all happened so fast I thought a bat had come into the house. He was unharmed by his plunge into the cellar, but was so embarrassed by his stupidity that it was an hour or more before he could come upstairs again. The antics of a Siamese are amusing, even in their old age. They're "on" every minute of their lives.

While a neutered male Siamese will usually come home at night, the protective tendency still exists when property lines are violated. In other words, they don't stop fighting just because they are indifferent to female Siamese. They no longer fight over them, but they will find other reasons just as valid.

The Siamese, however, is not innately vicious. They are generally more tolerant than other cats. Like children, they will respond to their environment and the manner in which they have been raised. They will become whatever is expected of them.

The Siamese's demands are voiced in a howling wail that cannot be ignored for any length of time. Whether they want to be let into a room, out of a closet, given something to eat, or just loved, they will wail without stopping until they get it. If we board our cat for a week while we take a vacation, he comes home hoarse and exhausted. His meow has a scratchy quality from overuse. Even though he is caged at the kennel with his long-haired "brother," this is not enough. The longhair accepts the situation, but the Siamese cannot bear the separation from home and family.

Life with an old Siamese is tranquil and quiet. Life with a young one is full of never-ending surprises. Nothing is ever the same once you have acquired one. In the kingdom of cats they are unique.

Manx

If you have noticed that your short-haired cat has no tail, you may be wondering whether you have a

Manx or an ordinary cat with its tail chopped off. There are other physical differences, however, that will lead to its true identity.

The Manx is sometimes called the "bunny cat" because of its strong back legs that are longer than the front legs and cause him to run with a hop. There is a hollow on its body where the tail should have been, and the hindquarters are noticeably higher than the frontquarters. The Manx has a large, round head with prominent cheekbones. He has a compact appearance although he is a foreign cat, not a domestic. Usually shy and sweet, the Manx is the clinging vine of the cat hierarchy and very attached to his owner. He makes a docile pet, and has a very soft voice.

Rex

Strange indeed is the cat with curly hair that wags its tail like a dog. Certainly these unusual characteristics are outstanding enough to attract your immediate attention, so you will not be surprised to learn that your cat is a Rex. These extraordinary mutants took several cat owners by surprise a number of years ago when they began to show up one at a time in otherwise normal litters of kittens. By breeding sons back to mothers, sisters to brothers, the breed was created, stabilized, and recognized.

Not only do they have curly hair, but curly whiskers and eyebrows as well. Through outbreeding, the Rex can be reproduced in any color, or pattern, even Siamese. The genetic mutation that makes the hair curly also limits the fur to one coat instead of the usual three that all other cats have. Because of this he is not waterproof and will literally become soaked to the skin in a rainfall.

Rex has a muted voice, and while they are descended from Domestic Shorthairs, they have a foreign body type. They have tremendous appetites and will eat unusual things such as milk chocolate, scampi, and cheese. Chances are if your cat happens to be a Rex, you will know it by now. If, in spite of all these clues, you still have doubts, offer him a bite of your candy bar.

Other Overwhelming Possibilities

There are several unusual short-haired breeds, such as the steerlike, sable brown Burmese that is closely related to the Siamese but not nearly as demanding, and the Havana Brown, another brown cat produced from a cross between a Domestic Shorthair and a Siamese, which is also foreign in appearance with chartreuse eyes.

Another short-haired breed with a difference is the Abyssinian. Their coats may be ticked with black or brown formed by two or three bands of color on each hair, much like that of a rabbit, or they may be a deep shade of red. They most closely resemble the ancient cats of Egypt with long bodies and whiplike tails. Their personality

43

traits are contradictory. Some say that they have remarkable memories and a great sense of humor. Others claim that they are as undisciplined as children.

Another exotic cat that is sometimes identifiable is the short-haired Foreign White, which is closely aligned to the Siamese in type and build. It is a long, sleek Oriental-type cat with no points or markings, a result of the dominant white genes that prevail in cats.

There are also Russian Blues (sometimes called Maltese) and British Blues, which differ from each other in the following ways. The hair of the Russian cat is bright blue with silver tips, and the thick coat stands away from the body instead of lying snugly against it. The British Blue is an exotic lavender-blue which may take as long as two years to develop. Actually, it frequently takes a couple of months for any kitten's coloring to become well defined, and breeders do not register a cat until it has matured enough to establish certainty of color.

Kitty's Coat of Many Colors

Now that you've decided whether you have a longhair or a shorthair (this didn't take long), your unregistered wanderer can be further identified by describing his color. Breeders and fanciers attribute certain personality characteristics to certain colors of the same breed, but we shall discount this. Chances are whatever kind of cat has selected you will develop to your personal specifications.

Both longhairs and shorthairs come in virtually the same colors, starting with self colors. With few exceptions, all longhairs must have orange or copper eyes to be show material. Naturally these are the most prized. Yellow eyes are permissible in some of the short-haired breeds. Siamese, Himalayans, and Whites must have blue eyes, and some cats may even be show material with "odd eyes," *i.e.*, eyes of two different colors. Green eyes are generally associated with wildcats so they are not acceptable in show cats, but green-eyed household pets can be enchanting.

Solid-colored cats begin with the aristocrat of all, white. However, white cats with blue eyes are sometimes deaf. The deaf cat can live a relatively unrestricted life in the country, but the hazards of city life may prove dangerous if he can't hear. The deaf cat will respond to vibrations on the floor if you want to get his attention, and he will recognize certain manual signs, but he doesn't read lips. He can learn to understand hand movements for suggestions such as Come, Eat, or No.

White cats frequently have orange eyes. A white cat with any eye color except blue will not be deaf. White cats with odd eyes, one blue and one orange, may be deaf on the side with the blue eye, but will hear with the ear above the orange one. If a blue-eyed white cat has even a few colored hairs on his body, his hearing will be normal. Since cats usually have extremely sensitive auditory skills, it will not be difficult to determine whether your blue-eyed white is deaf.

Black is probably the second most popular solid color. Black cats fade in the sun, giving the coat a rusty haze and making them undesirable as show material. They also generate a lot of electricity, particularly in cold weather. In fact, if you stroke your black cat in a dark room when the temperature is around 0° F. and the air is dry, you will see sparks. Put this on your list of entertaining things to do during the next winter blackout.

Other self, or solid, colors are blue, red, cream, brown, lilac, chocolate, and silver. Solid colors obviously do not take a noodle of knowledge to describe or identify. In fact, you probably already know whether you have a black or a red cat.

In addition to the solid colors, there are also sex-linked colors. These are the blue-creams, the tortoiseshells, and the calicos. Because of the white dominance, calicos are more common than tortoiseshells. Through the mystery of genetics, they are largely female. There is an occasional male born, but it will probably be sterile. These lovely species have been developed by the breeders for their unusual coats and coloring. The blue-creams are well patched in America, but a British blue-cream is brindled with no solid patches.

The tortoiseshell is patched in three colors, red, cream, and black. Each patch is distinct with no overlapping or tabby markings, and the colors are brilliant. They frequently have a cream- or red-colored blaze running up the nose and forehead (a blaze is an attractive marking that appears to divide the head in half).

The calico has a patched coat of black, red, and cream, like the tortoiseshell, but it is interspersed with white. The white appears on the chest, belly, legs, feet, and in the blaze on the nose.

The true red tabby is sometimes mistakenly referred to as a ginger or marmalade cat. Actually the ginger cat's fur is less red and more sandy-orange, but the ginger cat its truly a ginger cat, not an imitation red tabby.

The other coloring, albeit rather unusual in domestic house cats, is called ticking. This indicates a tip of color at the very end of the cat's fur. Red or silver ticking is seen occasionally in certain varieties of show cats.

You can now pick the color or colors that most closely describe your cat. Because of the dominant white gene that prevails in cats, yours will very possibly have a portion of white in his coat, particularly on his underside, but he will carry patches of his past on the other parts of his body. His colorful history will be displayed for you to read.

Patterns, Patches, and Polydactyls

If your long-haired kitty is two different colors equally divided, he is a bicolor. Black and white bicolors are called Magpies. Bicolors also come in blue and white, orange and white, and cream and white. Ideally your bicolor will not be striped or spotted but will be a 50–50 concentration of two distinct colors without brindling or overlap. Show standards require that a bicolor have white feet, neck, forelegs, chin, and lips with a white blaze on his face, over the top of his head, and running into and blending with the white at the back of his skull.

Most of our household cats have tabby markings. In the standard for the breed these come in two different patterns, blotched and striped. Tabby comes from the word *attabi* which was used to describe watermarked silks from Bagdad; this is the kind of pattern the tabby has. The base color will be overlayed with darker-color lines forming a distinct pattern.

The striped tabby is tiger striped with the stripes running vertically from the spine to the stomach. The striped tabby is dominant over the blotched tabby, so many of our household pets (the progenies of chance) will carry some sign of these stripes in the patches of color on their bodies. Show standards dictate that the dominant white be bred out of the pedigree tabby, but our precious pets, being unaware of this judgment, carry it proudly.

The blotched tabby will be covered in a swirling pattern that has a Rorschach quality. The pattern is divided down the middle of the cat and will be the same on each side. Tabby will have butterfly markings on his back, two bands across his chest like a necklace (these are called Lord Mayor's Chains in England), two long ovals with a patch in the middle on each flank, a ringed tail with a solid tip, and bracelets around his legs. The markings on your tabby's back may say Eat At Joe's Diner, but he's trying. Bear in mind that these are show standards, so if your pet has one out of six he's doing all right. The perfect tabby also has the letter *M* emblazoned on his forehead. Tabbies show up in a wide variety of colors (as the tabby patches on your cat will attest) such as brown, red, silver, and blue.

Spotted cats are close to the tabby. The base color will be spotted with a darker shade most easily observed when the cat is in motion. In a reclining position the spotted cat may look like a striped tabby.

If your cat is striped, he is a tabby striped; if he carries striped patches, he is a tabby patch. If he has orange, black, and cream patches on his white fur, he is a she and a calico. Tortoiseshell and calico refer to both color and pattern. If your long-haired cat has two colors, one of which is white, he is a bicolor. If he has points, he is probably a Siamese or a Himalayan, depending on the length of his hair. If his hair is curly, which is most unlikely, he's a Rex. Your cat may also be spotted or ticked, and he may have a blaze going up from his nose.

In addition, if your cat has six toes he is a polydactyl. This is a genetic mutation, and once it gets into a blood line, it stays. When polydactyls begin to appear in any geographic area of the country, they will proliferate and become ordinary. In the part of Connecticut where I live, they are quite common. These big-footed felines look like they're wearing galoshes. If, when your cat extends his claws, his feet are the size of tennis rackets, you might count his toes. He probably has six, and this extremely sophisticated description would befit his unusual condition.

As you can see, your cat doesn't need a pedigree to be worthy of an elegant description or to have a little class. He is what he is, and whatever he is, there's a word for it.

CHAPTER 4

Welcome Home, Kitty

Since you are not a mother cat, you should not carry your new kitty by the scruff of the neck. You can place your hand gently under his chest, holding his legs firmly with your fingers, and let the other hand support what's left over by cupping it around his hindquarters. You can teach other members of the family to handle him in the same manner.

The best way to bring the new creature home is in a small box (no lid, please, it's frightening). The best way to bring a full-grown cat home (this is rarely necessary since they usually come to you and are home the minute they arrive) is in a cat carrier. A cat carrier is a well-ventilated, enclosed box large enough for your adult cat to turn around in. It should have a sturdy carrying handle. Your cat can

51

go anywhere in this box and hardly know he's been there since visibility is not that great. It is ideal for trips to and from the vet, the kennel or cattery if he must be boarded, or for any kind of travel. Ideal, that is, for you—possibly a little less than that for the kitty who does not relish confinement. This will prevent him from interfering with the proper manipulation of the automobile by sticking his neck through the steering wheel or trying to ride in the driver's lap. In any event, it is the safest and most expedient means of transporting a cat from one place to another. These carriers are available at pet shops in a variety of shapes, sizes, materials, and prices.

Since it is probably your new kitten's first ride in a car, he will be justifiably frightened and threatened by the separation from his mother and siblings. The greatest reassurance you can give him is your voice, speaking softly to him as you gently stroke his back. It will help to alleviate some of the trauma of the strange new world he is about to enter. Bear in mind that he has been wrenched from the security of his past to come live with a total stranger. He doesn't like it, but you will quickly win him over with your winsome ways and a little warm milk.

When you arrive home and get your kitten safely inside, the rest of the family, including the other animals in the household, will want to inspect the new resident. This is best done under close supervision. Presumably other pets in the house have learned to obey your commands so they can be warned to be gentle. Your kitten will quickly reinforce your orders with a bat of its small, clawed paw if anything with fur comes too close. During these first few hours, the kitten will be frightened and suspicious. Stand by in case a donnybrook erupts, although this is unlikely. Kitty may be small, but the sound of his already well-developed hiss and the sting of his claws will keep the largest St. Bernard at arm's length.

Children and adults will want to take turns holding the kitten. This should be discouraged, but telling everyone to look, not touch, is unrealistic. As the kitten is passed from one to the other, he will enjoy a brief moment of security with each. Once this initiation is over, his apprehension can be eased with a little warm milk and a nap. After that give him a chance to recover and investigate his new surroundings. He's been through a lot, and tolerated more than most humans would. Each time he awakens he will be a little more at home in his new environment.

What Shall We Call Him?

The first question that will greet you as you come through the door is, "What are we going to call him?" Naming the cat is half the fun, although it is not unusual for a cat to live its whole life known as nothing more than Cat or Pussycat. Perhaps the following suggestions will provide a springboard from which you can take off:

POPULAR CAT NAMES

Butterball	Meow	Scratchy
Catnip	Morris	Tabby
Cupcake	Muffin	Tiger
Felix	Peep	Timmy
Frisky	Puff	Tom
Fritz	Sam	Whiskers

DESCRIPTIVE CAT NAMES

Bib	Goldy	Sandy
Blackie	Heather	Silver Top
Boots	Jumbo	Smokey
Buffy	Marmalade	Snowdrop
Cobby	Midge	Spice
Daffodil	Misty	Sunshine
Feather	Patches	Tiny
Fluffy	Princess	Tippy
Ginger	Pumpkin	Titan

PERSONALITY NAMES

Attila	Hamlet	Nijinsky
Buster	Isadora	Oepidus
Cleopatra	Lothario	Ollie
Don Juan	Madame Pompadour	Raisa
Elton	Mary Poppins	Rockefeller
Elvis	Matilda	Shake-speare
Esmé	Mehitabel	Solomon

Felix	Musetta	Sultan
Garfield	Napoleon	Tanya
Goldfinger	Nicodemus	Victoria

FAMOUS PAIRS

Adam & Eve	Mickey & Minnie
Amos & Andy	Nancy & Ron
Bonnie & Clyde	Oscar & Felix
Ginger & Fred	Rodgers & Hammerstein
Jack & Jill	Sears & Roebuck
Laurel & Hardy	Sonny & Cher
Lerner & Lowe	Wag & Puff

Until he learns his name (this could take awhile), he will answer nicely to Kitty, Kitty, Kitty, especially if you arc filling his food bowl as you say it.

High Tea, Low Tea, and Tuna

Now that your kitten has a happy home and a nice name, your next concern will be his cuisine. If the kitten is between seven and eight weeks old, he may need four or five small meals a day and a little warm milk. Milk should never be given cold to any cat. Because of its rapid growth rate, the kitten needs more protein and a higher caloric intake than a full-grown cat. This should continue until he is eight or nine months old when both growth and activity begin to slow down. He can be fed prepared canned foods with some extra canned fish, baby foods, especially meats, and a one-minute egg yolk in his warm milk. By the time he is four months old, he will only need two meals a day. The adult cat should be fed solid food twice a day, early in the morning and early in the evening. While it is not necessary for violins to accompany feeding time, the bowls and the area where he eats should be kept clean and pleasant.

Since cats are carnivores, wildcats and feral cats kill smaller animals for food. They eat the entire kill—viscera, flesh, and bones. This includes the contents of the victim's stomach at the time of his sudden demise, such as grass. In this way, the unsupervised cat automatically gets a well-balanced diet even though some of it may be secondhand. Maintaining a cat as a pet puts the responsibility of its diet on the owner. In other words, your meals must be as appealing and nutritious as a dead mouse.

A cat's nutritional needs are similar to ours, except cats need more protein. This should comprise approximately 30 percent of the cat's total intake. The diet should consist of the five basic elements of nutrition:

Protein (meat, fish, eggs, and cheese) Carbohydrates (sugar and starch)
Fat (meat, butter, whole milk)
Minerals (small quantities of calcium, phosphorus, iodine, and iron)
Vitamins (small quantities that can be found in green vegetables, eggs, fresh fish, liver, and brewer's yeast)

Cats are not finicky eaters if their owners do not make them that way. Carefully selected, commercially prepared cat foods assure your cat of a nutritionally balanced diet. These may be supplemented by table scraps, such as bites of meat, mashed potatoes, and vegetables, but these foods should not constitute more than one quarter of his total intake or they can destroy the balance the prepared food offers. The large manufacturers of prepared foods devote substantial amounts of money to research on nutrition, and their know-how is reflected in the product. A breakdown of the content of the food will appear on all packaging.

Dry cat food offers your cat what he needs and may be fed either as it comes from the bag, or moistened with water. Vitamins and minerals have been added, and the content listing indicates whether or not it has the required 30 percent protein. An added advantage to the convenience of dry food is that it can be left in the cat's bowl all day. Unlike dogs, who will turn over garbage cans and clean out the refrigerator, then show up for their evening meal as usual, cats have a tendency to eat only if they're hungry, and frequently leave food in the bowl.

Specialty cat foods have a 95 percent protein content, but will not meet all your cat's nutritional needs even though vitamins and minerals are added. They are an addition to the regular diet that can be mixed with your cat's regular dry meal. They come in such varieties as liver, chicken, tuna, mackerel, and sardines.

Maintenance cat foods should have the same well-rounded nutritional value as the dry meal. These canned foods provide total nutrition for the adult cat, but may not give your kitten all that he needs. Read the label carefully. If you have a male cat there are additional factors to consider. See page 81.

Another prepared food that is available is soft-moist cat food in sealed packages. It combines the flavor and appeal of the specialty foods with the nutrition and convenience of dry meal. One packet provides one feeding.

An 8- to 12-pound adult can eat four to seven ounces of food daily with a minimum of 30 percent protein. By experimenting with these varieties of foods and flavors, you will discover what your cat prefers. Chances are excellent that he will like all of them. A mixture of dry meal, specialty foods, and table scraps can titillate the palate of any cat who has never known the luxury of diced kidneys.

If you are inclined to prepare special menus for your cat, be my guest. He will be happy with cooked chicken (no skin), pork, and fish, all carefully boned, raw liver, beef, organ meats, horsemeat, veal, and lamb. In addition, he should also have some green vegetables, either raw or cooked (he'll probably prefer grass to green beans), a one-minute egg yolk twice a week, a little cheese and mashed potatoes.

Fresh water should always be available to your cat. If there is a community bowl for all the animals in the house, your cat may not care to drink from the same dish. It is therefore a good idea to give the cat his own water dish.

Vitamin and mineral supplements should not be necessary if your cat has a well-balanced, commercially prepared diet. In fact, these supplements can throw the balance off if not carefully administered. Proper feeding will give your cat good health and a long life.

Kitty's Other Needs

Your cat needs a special place to call his own. It can be a box or basket lined with clean cloth and a cushion or a French Provincial, four-poster bed. Cats like privacy and seclusion when they sleep, so this should be placed away from the center of activity in your house. The cat will sleep in his bed sometimes, but there are other places he will choose as well. A favorite spot is invariably an unmade bed. The unmade bed is attractive to cats because they love to nest in blankets.

In the winter cats love to stretch out or curl up in the sun. In the summer, if they are outdoor cats, they find cool, hidden places under shrubs where they can sleep undisturbed for hours. Whether your cat is an indoor cat or an outdoor cat, he should not be kept in the basement at night as this induces respiratory diseases and rheumatism. Outside of that, a cat can have sweet dreams just about any place he happens to be.

One of the most important points in cat care is the litter box. The litter box should be large enough to accommodate the whole cat. It should be lined with sawdust, sand, wood shavings, shredded paper, or commercial, deodorized kitty litter, which is probably the easiest and best method. The litter should be about two inches deep inside a shallow plastic or enamel pan. Cat excrement should be removed every day with a sieve. Once a week the litter box should be emptied and washed, and new litter put inside. Occasionally your cat may miss its mark, so a layer of newspaper around the floor outside the box is a good idea. As your cat grows, he may become trained to the outside, but it's still a good idea to keep a litter box in the house for emergencies or inclement weather.

The young kitten will have to be shown where the litter box is, but won't need any lengthy explanations as to its purpose. Cats are instinctively clean, and not only want to go to the bathroom away from their living quarters, but bury it as well. Once kitty knows where the box is, he will use it.

Your cat will also need a place to stretch and trim his claws. The house is full of possibilities for this, such as furniture and rugs, but the idea is to direct his attention elsewhere. For this purpose, he needs a scratching post. The best scratching post is a split log placed horizontally on the floor so the cat can get on it to stretch and scratch; or it can be vertically attached to a base like an indoor tree. A little catnip sprinkled on it may entice him away from the furniture.

Many people make or buy scratching poles covered with carpeting, but some cat authorities do not recommend this. They maintain that the cat cannot differentiate between the carpeting on the pole and that on the floor. My cats can tell the difference and refuse to use the pole. We have hairy rugs and furniture, and a scratching post that's never been used. I suggest using a split log.

The cat who goes outdoors will not necessarily confine his scratching to nature. After two hours of total freedom in the woods, our Siamese will come in and sharpen his claws on a living-room chair. The alternative to this is declawing, but it is not recommended. This is discussed further in Chapter 6. It should be emphasized again that not all cats are offenders, but if you want your house to be pristine, remember that your cat comes with no guarantee that he will avail himself of the scratching post.

Your cat, whether it is a longhair or a shorthair, should be brushed daily to remove dead hair from its coat. Special combs and brushes for each type of cat are available at pet shops. The long-haired cat needs more attention than the shorthair, and should be carefully combed and brushed once or twice a day. The cat will take care of his own cleansing, but in so doing, if the old hair has not been removed from his coat, he will swallow it and develop hair balls, which are harmful to digestion and generally uncomfortable.

The daily needs of your cat are therefore met with five basic things:

1. Three bowls (milk, water, and food)
2. A box or basket for a bed
3. Litter box
4. Scratching post
5. Grooming brush and comb

Once your cat knows where these things are (with the exception of the grooming brush and comb) he will practically train himself, and his care can be entrusted to a child. Cats are easy pets to keep happy and healthy.

Indoors and Out

Whether your cat will be allowed to explore the outdoors or not may depend largely on the quality of the environment where you live. If you live in a city apartment, his outdoor living may be confined to a collar and leash. A cat can be trained for this, provided the training is begun when he is very young. If you live in the city, your cat will enjoy sitting in open windows. It is very important that these windows have screens. Cats have excellent balance, but they have been known to fall; so every precaution must be taken to prevent such an accident.

If you live in a single dwelling in a rural or suburban neighborhood away from the highway or busy streets, your cat may have more unsupervised freedom. If your cat is going to be allowed to go outdoors, you can start taking the kitten out under your supervision as soon as you get him. He will not go far away from you, and he will love every minute of exploration. If you take him out for play periods several times a day, he will begin to learn the ways of the world. Your protection will be necessary for a few weeks, but it won't be long before he can go out unescorted. Cat intelligence prevails, and they will not take on more than they can handle.

A young cat will frequently run up a tree or telephone pole for the fun of it. He climbs to the top enthusiastically, only to look down and wonder how he got there. The ascent was easy, but from this great height he cannot piece together the reverse mechanics. Should he run down head first, or back down gingerly? Neither idea appeals to him, although he may make a feeble attempt at both. Finally fear and frustration give way to howling. You will instinctively try to lure him down with food at the base of the tree. He'll only howl louder because he can't get it.

The next thing is to call the fire department. The fire department will refer you to one of the animal societies who will tell you that your cat will come down of his own accord. One woman called the fire department to get her cat out of a tree and was informed that they rescued people, not cats. They tried to assuage her concern by telling her there were no instances of cat skeletons being found in treetops, which was a good indication that the cat would come down of its own accord. The woman was not satisfied so she called a steeplejack. He then presented her with a bill for $100. While your pet is worth that and more, it is an unnecessary expenditure. The cat isn't going to fall from the tree because he's holding on for dear life. However, until he is so hungry he can't stand it, he will not get himself out of this predicament—and cats can go a long time without eating. He may even spend the night in the tree. Nevertheless, he will work it out, and both you and your cat will survive the ordeal.

Young kittens love to play. There are a number of rubber toys, such as mice and balls, that will amuse them for hours. A wooden spool, a couple of unshelled walnuts, a piece of paper on a string hung from a doorknob or pulled about a room will also entertain your cat. There are soft toys filled with catnip. Catnip makes cats frisky. Kittens won't need it—they're active enough—but it can make old cats act like kittens when they smell it, eat it, or roll in it.

Outdoors in the early evening, when moths and flying creatures are about, your kitten will jump and frolic with anything that moves. He is a miniature of the fearless lion or tiger pouncing, and leaping, and darting around the jungle of your lawn. He is beginning to establish his boundaries and reign supreme.

CHAPTER 5

Training Tabby before Tabby Trains You

The most crucial thing to remember about training a cat is timing. Once a kitten or cat has developed certain behavior patterns, they cannot be easily modified. As pointed out earlier, this is one of the advantages of getting a kitten rather than an older cat that has been trained by somebody else.

It is very easy to train a cat in basic household conduct. You have nothing more to do than show him where to eat, where his litter box is, and where to sleep, and he will be happy to go along with whatever you have established. If you remove the litter box in order to train your cat to the outdoors, he may still return to the spot where the box was to relieve himself. Since it was acceptable originally, he will not understand why the absence of the box makes it less so. The litter box may have to stay.

Dogs can be taught to do almost anything by spanking them with a folded newspaper, and rewarding them with a morsel of food. This isn't true of cats. They won't toss aside their dignity for a bite of food. Besides, newspaper punishment will only frighten a cat and make him timid in the presence of the punisher. He is totally unaware of his misdeed since it was a natural response for him. If the cat makes a "mistake" in a corner of the dining room, you can't show it to him and reprimand him as you would a dog. He didn't hide it in the corner because he knew it was wrong and was ashamed; he used the corner so he would not attract attention to such a delicate moment. If your cat makes a mistake in the house, try to consider why. Maybe his litter box was out of place; maybe it was dirty; maybe he told us he wanted out and we didn't pick up on the signal. In any event, we figure out what *we* did wrong.

The cat's cerebellum controls automatic activities such as defecating, urinating, and sleeping. It also controls natural body responses to external stimuli. Memory and conscious actions are located in the cerebrum, which is quite small in lower animals. It is in the cerebrum where memory training takes place. Each time an animal successfully connects with what is expected of him during training, the next lesson is that much easier to learn. Therefore, as our cats get older, they learn more easily. This is why they seem to understand what we say to them after several years of being with us. Without our realizing it, they are beginning to recognize more words that we say to them. According to Dr. Leon F. Whitney in his book, *The Complete Book of Cat Care*, our pets do not live long enough to develop their full potential. If you are living with an old cat who has been your companion for a number of years, you will virtually be able to hold a conversation with him. At this rate, if a cat's life could be extended another twenty years, it is quite feasible they could become meter readers, security guards, or government officials.

Roll Over and Play Dead

The average household cat has a very limited repertoire of tricks. It requires endless patience to teach a cat to do tricks, partly because most of them won't perform for a potato chip, and partly because they are too independent to care. A cat's best responses occur when what you tell him to do coincides with what he feels like doing at the moment.

We have a black, long-haired cat the size of the average Cocker Spaniel. When we say *speak* to him in a squeaky little voice, he will try to imitate the sound and *peep* back at us. We're not sure if we learned it from him, or vice versa, but his response is unfailing. On the other hand, we are constantly telling our Siamese to shut up, and all he does is growl back at us. However, both of our cats have developed definite inflections and histrionics which give one the eerie feeling that they are trying to talk.

The longer you keep your cat, the more like you he will become. The more he is handled, the less he will resent it. The more he is talked to, the more he will try to talk back to you. The more he is loved, the more loving he will be.

When your cat learns to recognize his name, he will respond by giving you his undivided indifference. This is one of his better tricks. As long as canned food is part of his diet, he will miraculously materialize at the sound of the electric can opener. Never mind this roll over and sit stuff. If good manners and an adorable personality are enough for you, you'll find training your cat presents no problem—just do whatever he says.

Bird Killers

Some cats are bird killers; others are not. I think some are smart enough to eat the birds on the spot, or leave them where they are. Since cats are carnivorous, the killing of small animals and birds for food is instinctive. However, if your cat is well fed it's unlikely he'll kill because he's hungry. While it is difficult to get into ego psychology with a low-verbal cat, I do not believe that they are out to kill if their stomachs are full, and they know where the next meal is coming from.

A cat at play can be very enthusiastic. Bird killing, when not done out of necessity, probably begins as a game. A cat sees something moving (a small bird or rabbit) and he starts batting it around in fun. The more the victim struggles to escape (the cat will give him a head start to keep the sport going), the more excited the cat becomes. When the "toy" stops moving, if the cat's appetite is whetted, he may eat what he has killed, but more likely than not he will carry the dead mouse, mole, rabbit, or bird home and leave it outside the door. If he were killing for food he would have devoured it in the field, but I like to think he brought it home and left it where he could play with it again, not knowing that its playing days are over.

A bell can be placed on a stretchable collar around the cat's neck. (The elasticity enables him to extricate his head if he gets caught on a tree or bush.) The sound of the bell will warn birds and small animals of the cat's approach. However, there are times when your outside cat must hide from his own pursuers, and the bell will reveal his slightest movement. If your cat has a bell around its neck, you will always know where he is, but so will the dog next door. You may save a bird and lose a cat.

While I've never heard of a cat's being carried off by birds, birds will attack cats. If a cat has been particularly troublesome to a group of birds during the day, when their leader returns in the evening they will swoop down on the unsuspecting cat as he walks across the lawn. Cats have an amazing instinct about their own limitations, and the cat who is being attacked by diving birds will not look up for fear of having an eye pecked out, but he may try to hide by flattening his body in the grass. The birds will screech and dive and go through fearless motions of pecking at the cat's head which they never quite touch, but the cat is scarcely disturbed, let alone frightened, by their antics. It is a noisy, albeit painless, revenge, but the truth is birds *do* attack cats. Tell *that* to the next bird lover who tries to have your cat arrested!

A cat is cautious by nature and will not overextend itself or tempt fate. It is inevitable that he will fight with other cats, but this, too, is a sport. For the most part he is going to come to terms with his environment.

Stick With Me, Baby, and I'll Make You a Star

All of us have seen cats on television commercials, in the movies, and photographed on the pages of magazines. The most famous of these commercial cats is Morris, an ordinary, finicky fellow with whom everyone can relate. These are special cats who are specifically trained for careers in the lights.

The career cat's temperament is more important than his looks. He has to be friendly, gentle, and undisturbed by loud or unexpected noises. He must be completely secure with an abiding trust in his handler. He must be trained to come when called, to leap from a specific height, and to sit in a posed position. Do you think it's easy? Mrs. P. Chapman of Great Britain, who does this sort of thing, has several suggestions on how a cat can be trained for television.

The first thing is to appeal to his greed. Be sure that he is enticed and rewarded with food. To teach the cat to sit, you place an article of your own clothing on a table, then sit the cat on it, settling him gently as you caress him with your voice and hands. Slowly back away encouraging the cat to stay where he is. Eventually the cat will understand what is wanted of him and will remain seated on the table. Teaching the cat to walk to a certain point is accomplished by placing a plate of food at the desired destination; the greedy cat will be happy to come.

The cat will learn to leap by being placed on top of a tall, secure ladder, then gently nudged closer and closer to the edge until he jumps of his own accord. Again, each time he makes the leap he should be rewarded with food. The height can be increased as he becomes more adept.

The commercial television cat is often called upon to select the sponsor's bowl of food over three inferior brands. Mrs. Chapman does not reveal how this is accomplished, but assures us that it can be done.

Since cats are sometimes required to play their big scene out of doors, they increase their value considerably if they are not distracted by the sounds and movements around them. The cat must also be trained to come on call, or he may very well walk off the set.

Superstar cats should be handled as much as possible and exposed to people at every opportunity, the same as show cats. They should get used to wearing a collar, a sweater, or a tiara around the house. It's not all roses and encores. The cat must be a good traveler since all his work is done on location, and must be able to withstand the rigors of a frequently interrupted routine. Mrs. Chapman further points out that if your superstar has a stand-in, another cat of the same size and color, with an equally serene disposition, it will save a lot of wear and tear on the star while lighting and cameras are being adjusted. There's no business like show business.

Fly Me

The best way to travel with a cat is put it in a kennel and forget the whole idea. Unless your cat is trained to travel in the car from kittenhood, he is not an ideal companion on the road. A cat that is not used to the car won't adapt to riding to the vacation cottage once a year.

However, it is sometimes necessary to travel with the cat, and this is best done by putting it in a cat carrier. While the cat may eventually settle down in the automobile if he is allowed to be free, there is always the danger of his getting out through an open window or door. Cats move fast and it's not always possible to stop them. The cat should not be fed before traveling, and should be given an opportunity to familiarize himself with his carrier before confinement.

In our mobile society, where we are frequently uprooted, it is necessary to ship pets—usually by plane. This can be handled by your moving company, which will provide the necessary shipping cases or carriers. Unfortunately, the animals are not always met at the other end of the line as they should be. Unless arrangements have been made in advance with a kennel owner, to meet them and keep them until the rest of the family arrives, it can be heartbreaking to learn that your pet has been forgotten or misplaced for twenty-four hours. All arrangements should be carefully checked.

There is a better way. There are travel agencies for jet-set pets such as the Connecticut-based Cosmopolitan Canine Carriers, with offices in Stamford and Darien, will arrange for pickup and transportation to the airport, obtain necessary health documents on the animal, make all reservations, and appoint an associate or agent to meet the cat when it arrives at its destination. Whether your cat wants to go from Omaha to Peoria, or Omaha to Peru, Cosmopolitan Canine (800-243-9105) can handle it. If you are making a long-distance move, your moving company can be instructed to use the services of an animal-oriented travel agency, or you can do this yourself. It is a much more responsible means of transporting your pet.

If you are shipping your cat on your own, here are some travel tips:

1. Avoid DC-10 aircraft in warm weather because the pressurization prevents temperature stabilization in the hold.
2. Book your pet on a nonstop flight, thus avoiding plane changes which present another opportunity for your cat to be lost or misplaced
3. Make reservations in advance—only a limited number of animals are taken on each flight.
4. Don't feed your cat before the trip.
5. Let your cat become accustomed to the strangeness of his cat carrier before he is confined in it.

Few cats ever become seasoned travelers. They do not like the disruption in their lives; they are distrustful of the situation; they detest the separation from their owners. For these reasons you want to make his trip as swift and comfortable as possible.

CHAPTER 6

Keeping Kitty Well

A newborn kitten weighs about 3½ ounces. When mature, it will weigh between 9 and 17 pounds normally, but may weigh up to 28 pounds. It will be between 8 and 10 inches long.

The fattest cat on record, according to *The Guinness Book of World Records*, weighed 43 pounds. His name was Spice and he lived in Ridgefield, Connecticut. He was four times the size of the average cat. When Spice died just before his twelfth birthday, he had dieted down to 35 pounds, but because of his size he hadn't walked for a year prior to his death. At the animal hospital he stayed in a Great Dane's cage, and when he visited area schools to show the children what a real cat could become, he was pulled from room to room in a milk cart. Everybody loved him.

While there are no standard weight charts for cats as there are for their owners, if you can see your cat's ribs, it's too thin. If you can't feel its ribs, it's too fat. Obesity in cats is not healthy as it induces heart and joint diseases which decrease the animal's life span.

Cats live to be about fourteen years old, but sometimes make it to eighteen or nineteen. An unlikely few live to be thirty. One of these old-timers in Plymouth, Indiana, a cat named Christie Bell, lived to be thirty years old, but due to a slight case of rheumatism, she gave up tree climbing and stopped chasing birds in the last year or so. Her life span, according to her vet, would be comparable to that of a person 180 years old. It's almost certain that none of us would feel like chasing birds or climbing trees at that age. Most of my friends gave it up before they were forty.

Kittens lose their baby teeth when they are four or five months old. Mature adult cats will have thirty teeth, which they sometimes lose as they grow older.

Cats cannot see in total darkness, but they can see better at night than other animals or human beings. Their pupils dilate dramatically, allowing more light to come in. A cat's eyes reflect light at night because of a membranous layer of the retina called the tapetum.

A cat's whiskers, unlike a man's, are delicate

sense organs. Cats will touch whiskers to communicate with one another. Approximately 25 to 30 whiskers grow in four rows from the side of the mouth to above the eyes, each one attached to nerves in the skin. These feelers help them make their way through brush and bushes and keep them from bumping into things.

The most unique feature of the cat is its retractable claws. When a cat extends its legs, the paws automatically expand to an extraordinary size, and the claws will appear. The claws are retracted to protect them. During the course of a year a cat will shed its claws, and it is not unusual to find one around the house now and then. Unlike having a cat declawed, the shedding of claws is natural, and they are replaced by the equally natural growth of new ones. The claws are not only used for protection, but are responsible for the cat's exquisite balance and other physical feats he performs, such as climbing, stretching, and running.

Cats are by nature healthy and resilient. If properly fed and provided for, they are not a burden. The responsibility of caring for a cat has been summed up in a booklet entitled *The Cat's Rights* published by Pet Pride Press. These are as follows:

The Right to be clean;
The Right to be healthy;
The Right to his own veterinarian;
The Right to be protected from harm;
The Right to claim one human as his owner;

The Right to live in peace without fear;
The Right to live in a pleasant environment;
The Right to be free from harassment;
The Right to keep his own claws;
The Right to human companionship;
The Right to have a concentrated variety diet;
The Right to be free of parasites;
The Right of a female to be a spay;
The Right of a male cat to be a neuter;
The Right to purr out of happiness;
The Right to live his full fifteen years.

Health and Welfare

Never mind welfare. Your cat isn't eligible. His good health, however, is your responsibility. This begins with the kitten's first inoculation against feline distemper when he is six weeks old. The second of the two-series shots should be given when he is fourteen weeks with an annual booster thereafter. In addition to this, if the cat is allowed outdoors, he should be given an annual rabies shot any time after he is six months old.

Cats are subject to external parasites, such as fleas, lice, ticks, and ear mites. Fleas are the most common, are visible to the eye, and can be treated at home. The cat can be sprayed with flea powder outdoors so the dead fleas will fall on the ground, or he can wear a flea collar. However, the danger of the collar's getting caught on a tree or some other obstacle is always present. Flea powders are usually effective on lice as well. Lice are more difficult to see, but may be the reason why your cat is scratching.

If a cat shakes his head frequently, it probably signifies he has ticks or ear mites. A tick can be removed from the cat's ear with tweezers, but it is advisable to see your veterinarian if you think your cat has ear mites. A cat's ears are very sensitive so any problems should not go unattended.

There are a number of illnesses that your cat might conceivably fall prey to, but this is a matter for your veterinarian. Your job is to recognize your cat's symptoms of ill-health so you will know when he needs professional attention. The following are symptoms of a sick cat:

1. Changes in physical appearance, such as a rough coat, runny nose, or watery eyes.
2. Loss of appetite
3. Coughing
4. Vomiting
5. Diarrhea or constipation
6. Discomfort or bloody discharge with urination
7. Shivering. While this might only indicate that your cat is cold, frightened, or excited, it can also mean that he is sick.
8. Convulsions. These can be brought on by poisoning, brain damage, or infectious disease.
9. Lethargy. This may be hard to identify in an older, inactive cat, particularly in mid-winter when he normally becomes less active.

If any of these conditions persists for more than two days, it's time to see the vet. If your cat is particularly uncomfortable, he will hide under a piece of furniture, and stay there. His withdrawal in this or a similar fashion is a sure sign that something is wrong. Cats do not get sick often, but when they do, they need a doctor. Your responsibility is to recognize when your cat is not well so you can get him the professional care he needs.

Upper-respiratory infections, feline leukemia, and cystitis are the diseases most frequently seen by veterinarians. All three are serious and can be fatal. They require immediate attention and preventative measures.

Sneezing and a watery, puslike discharge from the nose and eyes may be the symptoms of a respiratory disorder. The presence of a cough, however, may signify pneumonia, which calls for prompt and intensive treatment. Since most of these respiratory disorders are highly contagious, most veterinarians prefer not to hospitalize the cat; they will be cared for at home under your vet's direction. The most severe cases of upper-respiratory infections are usually found where large numbers of cats are in contact with each other, such as boarding kennels or pet shops. Keeping your cat indoors and away from contact with other cats is the best precaution that can be taken against respiratory problems. If your cat is an outside animal, vaccines are available against feline rhinotracheitis and feline pneumonitis, although the effectiveness of both vaccines has not as yet been determined.

Feline leukemia is a fatal, cancerous disease that can only be diagnosed through laboratory tests. Since the disease is in the bloodstream, the cat will show signs of progressive weight loss, poor appetite, fever, and pale mucous membranes. As these symptoms may signal some other ailment, lab tests are the only reliable means of diagnosing the cat's problem. Without proper testing, feline leukemia can be confused with feline infectious anemia, which manifests similar symptoms. However, infectious anemia will usually respond to treatment with antibiotics and vitamin-mineral supplements. If your cat dies of either of these diseases, it is recommended that you wait a month before getting another cat, and dispose of all previous litter pans, feeding dishes, and bedding.

Male cats are frequently troubled by an obstruction in the urethra or urinary tract, technically called urolithiasis or cystitis. According to the latest research at Colorado State University funded by the Morris Animal Foundation in Denver, these obstructions are diet-induced by ash residue in the food. The study shows that a diet with 1.6 percent phosphorus, and 0.75 to 1 percent magnesium produces obstruction, the calculi formation being in direct proportion to the amount of magnesium and phosphorus in the diet. Calculi is thought to affect 10 percent of all male cats. Long-term research is now concerned with diet control of this problem and with the formulation of an additive to prevent the formation of these stones, which can be fatal.

Since it seems reasonable to conclude that these obstructions are diet-induced, there are several recommendations that may prevent their formation. The contents of the cat food you select should show the lowest percentage of ash possible—less than 3 percent ash maximum. If dry meal is fed to your cat, it should be moistened if there is any reason to believe he may have urinary problems. Some vets recommend that dry food not be used at all, but the question is moot. Many cats who have had a consistent diet of dry meal over a period of years are never troubled with blockage. Until the question is resolved, the best prevention is keeping the urinary tract clear and irrigated by encouraging the cat to drink water and making it available to him at all times. If you are suspicious of urinary irregularities, a pinch of salt may be added to the cat's food as this will make him drink more water. It is also suggested that foods containing large quantities of ground bones (such as fish products) be limited. Milk intake should also be restricted, or if given in small amounts, diluted half and half with water. In recurrent cases of cystitis, surgery is sometimes recommended to enlarge the urethral opening so that blockage will be less likely to occur. Any irregularities in your cat's urinary habits, such as the appearance of blood in the urine, call for *immediate* examination and treatment by a veterinarian.

Cats don't like medicine, but if you must administer it, it can be forced between the teeth with a medicine dropper by holding the cat's jaw. It may also be put on his food, or on his paw which he will lick clean.

Administering pills to your cat is a bit more challenging, but there is a recommended procedure for this. Sit the cat in front of you and grasp his head in your hand with your thumbs and fingers pressing from opposite sides of the upper jaw. Pull the head straight up with the nose pointing toward the sky, hold the lower jaw open, and drop the pill on the back of his tongue. This is best done by two people, one to hold the cat's mouth open, the other to drop the pill in place and give it a gentle push in the direction of the throat. Close the cat's mouth and hold it shut, gently massaging the throat to help the pill go down. Only on a veterinarian's orders should you give aspirin to your cat since it may be harmful to his stomach. Any medication, in fact, should only be given as prescribed.

A healthy cat has a pink tongue and a cold, moist nose. His coat will be soft and shiny, his appetite good, and he will be as frisky as weather and age permit. If he lacks this luster, he may need to be checked by your veterinarian. If you do not have one already, you might get a recommendation from the person from whom you got your cat, or ask a friend.

Declawing

Cats are comical characters. It's a source of constant amusement to watch a cat go through the process of daily living. They are fun to be around, but there are two things that must be taken seriously: one is declawing; the other is neutering or spaying.

A cat is not only physically afflicted by declawing, he is psychologically anguished. When a cat's claws are surgically removed to prevent his damaging furniture and carpets, he is deprived of his only defense and his most necessary tool for survival. Imagine yourself without fingernails or toenails and multiply both the suffering and the discomfort by a thousand. This is what the cat endures when he is declawed.

Inside the house the cat will not be able to maintain his footing on a slick floor. He has nothing with which to grasp so he can't jump or play in his customary manner. In addition to this, he has no means of protecting himself. He can become psychologically disturbed after declawing, or overly suspicious and defensive. His disposition can change so acutely that he must be caged and ultimately destroyed. It is an emotionally traumatic experience for the cat.

Cats' systems are more sensitive than ours. As a result, they cannot always be treated with painkillers. The declawing is painful surgery; recovery is slow. If the claws grow back, they may grow back through the top of the paw, creating new problems for the cat as this unnatural growth fosters the development of sores. Proper surgical procedures are geared to avoid this, but proper surgical procedure may not always be followed.

When the end digit, including the claw, is removed from a cat's paw, the sensory and motor nerves are damaged or destroyed. They do not mend easily, leaving the cat with numbness and tingling during the long convalescence. It is, after all, an amputation.

If we are threatened by our cat's claws, then it is better not to have a cat. If we love our cat and understand what he must go through, we will not declaw him for our convenience. He is a living creature who does not deserve to suffer at human hands.

How to Make a Good Cat Even Better

Neutering a cat is exactly that. He or she is not being deprived of his sex drive, but relieved of it. Upon being relieved of this unrelenting sex drive, your cat will become an ideal pet.

It is virtually impossible to live with a male cat that has not been neutered. He does not make a desirable pet. Because of his insatiable urges, the minute he is let out he will take off in search of love. His personality will be aggressive. He will be constantly engaged in fierce combat with other male cats for the favors of the female in heat. Inside the house he will spray on the walls and drapes, producing an obnoxious odor that cannot be covered up or removed. He will howl and yowl and be most disagreeable. Worst of all, he will prefer half the cat kingdom to you!

Neutering or castrating a male cat is a relatively

simple operation performed under general anesthetic when the cat is eight or nine months old. The male cat will mature between nine and twelve months, so it is wise to have the neutering performed before that time. Usually the cat stays in the hospital overnight. When you get him home, you will have a playful, nonagressive pussycat. The anxiety and stress that the sex urge dictated will evolve into an affection and compatibility between you and your cat. There are no adverse effects to the operation.

The female cat undergoes the same anguish as the male in her desire to procreate. From the time she matures (somewhere between five and eight months), she will come into heat every three or four weeks, although she will only be able to conceive two or three times a year. Nevertheless, each time she comes into heat, she will crave male companionship. If this is denied, she will be difficult to live with. If her needs are met, she could produce as many as fifteen kittens a year.

Spaying is the removal of the ovaries. Although the surgery requires an incision in the abdomen, it is not dangerous for a healthy cat. Most veterinarians recommend spaying female cats before their first heat, when they are about four or five months old. After a short stay in the hospital, she is entrusted to you. During convalescence, care must be taken so that the incision does not break open.

After surgery your female cat will be more lovable and far less restless. No longer a slave to her insatiable sex drive, she will be content with her surroundings. In addition to this, the spayed cat has a greater chance for a longer and healthier life. She will not develop pyometritis (uterine infection) or breast tumors, nor will her health be endangered by litters of kittens.

Other methods of birth control have been developed for animals, but they only prevent conception. They do not take away the desire. The only sure way to solve your cat's frustration is surgery. Every contented cat is an "it."

Rock-a-Bye, Kitty

The average period of gestation in cats is 65 days, but kittens can be born from 56 to 71 days after coition. In an uncontrolled situation the kittens may have more than one father, adding considerable variety to the litter. A female cat may be impregnated by more than one male and bear each of their kittens in one litter of four or five babies.

The unconfined, unspayed, female cat may not announce her intended motherhood until the kittens have arrived. You might look in a closet one morning and find her nursing three or four little kittens. It is easier to recognize a short-haired cat's pregnancy than that of a long-haired cat.

If you have determined that your cat is going to have kittens, but you're not sure when, she will let you know. During the last week of her pregnancy she will restlessly prowl the house seeking out a properly secluded place in which to give birth. This is when you come up with the maternity box. A large cardboard carton is fine. The entrance should have a barrier high enough to keep the kittens in, but low enough for the mother to get out. To assure privacy, and the darkness the kittens will require, the top of the box should be left on. The bottom should be soft and comfortable, covered with shredded newspaper and a towel. It must be large enough for the mother cat to stretch out on her side with plenty of room for nursing. The soon-to-be mother can be shown the box and placed in it, so she will recognize it for what it is.

The day before the cat delivers, her stomach will drop noticeably. Labor will be heralded by a slight vaginal discharge. If the cat has not already headed for the maternity box, you can lead her to it. It should be placed in an out-of-the-way spot that the cat would choose herself. The normal birth of four kittens will take two or three hours. As each one emerges, the mother will bite the umbilical cord, remove the membranous sack, and give the kitten its first vigorous bath to get its circulation and respiration functioning.

The mother cat should be inoculated against distemper and rabies, since this temporary immunity will be passed onto her kittens who could die of distemper before they were old enough for shots. During the latter stages of pregnancy, the cat should be given all she wants to eat. Her appetite will take on significant gains. Two or three days after the kittens arrive, her appetite will dwindle, but she should have access to her food and a good supply of fresh water. For the duration of her nursing period she should have all the food she wants. If she is not producing enough milk to feed her family, semimoist or canned food should be increased. If the problem persists, the veterinarian should be consulted.

When the kittens are three to four weeks old, they will begin nibbling at solid food which should be made available to them. Dry meal can be moistened, however, for the little ones.

The kittens will be weaned between seven and ten weeks. To decrease the pressure of the milk, the day the kittens are weaned all food should be removed from the mother cat. On the second day she should be fed one-quarter the normal amount, one-half on the third day, and three-quarters on the fourth day. By the fifth day she can return to her pre-pregnancy feeding schedule. The kittens will now be accustomed to solid food and milk from a saucer.

CHAPTER 7

If Your Pet Is, God Forbid, an Ocelot or a Margay

Several years ago, perhaps a decade or two, it was quite popular to adopt some of the more exotic cats for pets. These included cheetahs, ocelots, and margays. It was high fashion to be photographed walking down Fifth Avenue with a cat that looked like a panther. Then stories began circulating about these cats attacking children, or clawing their owners, and their popularity waned. Indeed, it is a frightening thing to consider the possibility of your cat grabbing you by the throat or removing one of your arms. However, for those of you who want to go beyond the comforts offered by a striped tabby or a blue Persian, jungle cats are available through pet stores on special order.

Patience

Both the margay and the ocelot need special care and understanding. It is recommended that you acquire a kitten under four months old, bearing in mind that it was born in the jungle, and lived there for four months prior to arrival in your home. It therefore has little understanding of human nature or urban living and will be particularly vulnerable to disease and stress.

Chances are the kitten will have been mishandled by the trappers who found him for you, and since this is the only treatment he has known from human beings, you do not come into the picture with everything in your favor. His responses will need restructuring. This can be done through kindness and patience, the key words in the care and training of a jungle cat. In addition to his negative treatment by humans, your kitten has undergone traumatic changes in diet, climate, and environment. He will be easily frightened.

You should have an agreement with the seller that the sale is contingent upon your vet's examination and approval. He will probably be suffering from malnutrition and/or rickets, so he will need immediate vitamin-mineral supplements that will provide high calcium intake. You should choose a vet who is experienced in treating and caring for exotic cats and have your cat checked for such things as ringworm, external parasites, general health, and psychological disorders.

Your exotic cat can then be fed ground, lean beef with a bit of fat for starters. Like any kitten, he needs several meals a day. A week or so later, depending on the age of the kitten when he arrives, he can eat diced meat chunks which can be increased in size as he grows. Raw meat is best for him, but he should not eat pork. Some cats enjoy celery, lettuce, and an occasional house-plant. It should be noted that milk, liver, kidneys, and canned foods can cause diarrhea.

Safety First

Your large kitten will get his permanent teeth when he is about five months old. In the event that all his baby teeth do not fall out, it may be necessary to let your vet remove them, along with his front claws. When the permanent teeth are in, it's time to remove or file down the canines. Your vet must perform this with the utmost care to avoid fracturing the cat's jaws. This is going to alter somewhat the shape of the cat's head, but it's better than altering the shape of your arm. Last but not least, the cat should be neutered at the age of ten to twelve months.

As your cat grows, you may discover that you have a large margay or a small ocelot. It is very difficult to tell the kittens apart at birth. You should avoid startling the cat, no matter what kind it is; its nervous system can't take the shock and it could have a coronary.

The Big Kitty Box

Jungle cats are harder to housebreak than domestic cats. It may take months to get them to use a pan, and in the meantime they are apt to use anything containing water, like the kitchen sink, the bathtub, or any large pot or pan convenient for relief. Sometimes they take it upon themselves to decide to simply forego the cat box altogether and use the toilet, a situation that might surprise an unexpected guest. If you are attempting to train your cat to a box, be sure it is not too shallow. Jungle cats urinate standing up. It is suggested that you use several litter boxes, possibly in every room, until he establishes the place he prefers.

If properly introduced, your jungle cat should get on well with your domestic cat. These animals, however, are not recommended for homes where there are children under ten years of age. These cats are playful, and the child must be large enough to cope with it.

Now for the good news. Your exotic cat will amply reward you for your patience and efforts in training and caring for him. They are extremely affectionate once they shed their innate wildness. They are also very playful and entertaining, but they are nocturnal and may keep you awake nights jumping back and forth across your bed. If this happens, and your health is threatened, you can make kitty's bed inside a cage, closing the door quickly when you want to sleep. They need a lot of play and enjoy all kinds of domestic-cat toys. They love to climb. Nothing will make your exotic cat happier than a six-foot stepladder in the living room, although it may do little to enhance your decor. They also like water, and can have loads of fun in a tub or a swimming pool.

Margays have a jolly way of lurking in playful ambush on top of doors, then jumping on the shoulders or head of the first person to walk through. Needless to say this is a little mind boggling until you get used to it, but it's all in fun and covered by Blue Cross.

Look Before You Leap

A final word of warning about exotic cats. It's not a capital idea to buy one that is advertised in the newspaper. If the present owner is getting rid of it, there's a reason, and this is the same reason you do not want to buy it. Instead of finding yourself with a little two- to four-month-old kitten, the advertised cat is probably about a year old. Chances are excellent that he is urinating in the sink, springing at the stereo from the chandelier, and displaying aggressive hostility toward everyone who comes into the home. Before you seriously consider getting such a spectacular pet, remember that if it doesn't work out, it may be harder to dispose of than the plague. If you are a sensitive, patient person, you could make a margay very happy. Otherwise, consider a canary.

CHAPTER 8

How to Live Happily Ever After with Plastic Furniture

Cats may not be for everyone. Allergies to their dander or irreversible cases of ailurophobia may make ownership unrealistic. However, if you have ever owned a cat without sneezing, you know the return you can expect on your investment. Dog may be man's best friend, but the cat is so reflective of its owner that he is more like an alter-ego.

Once you have the cat of your choice, you are eligible for membership in a cat club. Like most animal organizations, the meetings are for owners. There are a constantly growing number of cat clubs throughout the country, and your veterinarian, or another cat lover, can put you in touch with one in your area. Your cat doesn't have to be a papered pedigree for you to join the club—everyone is welcome. The only requirement is a strong affinity for cats. You might also want to subscribe to *Cats Magazine*. Between the club and the magazine you will keep current on diseases and cures, shows throughout the country, training problems, and all the other things that are of concern to conscientious cat owners.

Show Time

Many people enjoy showing their cats. The cats themselves are neither enthusiastic nor reluctant, but that's not surprising.

If you are a prospective cat owner, a visit to a show will amply reward you. For the small price of admission, it will give you an opportunity to see a wide variety of breeds that are representative of the cream of the cat kingdom. Most of the pedigreed cats in the show belong to breeders, and each cat will be a model for his standard. These are the elite. There is no doubt that you will find a cat here that will suit you.

The cats in a show are kept in individual wire cages and may be viewed throughout the day. Their color identity, breed, and name will be posted on the cage, and frequently the breeder will have a supply of business cards on hand. As the day goes on, ribbons and awards will begin to appear on the cats' cages after judging. The cats are indifferent to all of it, but their owners respond enthusiastically to the accolades.

The owners bring cloth covers to fit around the cages for privacy, and the interior design alone is worth the trip. Some of the cages are covered with cat-print fabrics. Others have a definite decor which may be anything from Louis Quatorze to Siamese Modern. The bottom of the cage might be covered with a rug or blanket, and there is a litter box in one corner. Many of the cages contain enamel bowls with crocheted liners where the cat can curl up and sleep. Colorful catnip toys dangle from the ceiling to alleviate kitty's boredom, and sometimes a favorite picture of the tenant is also on display.

When the cats are called for judging, they do not walk around in a ring as dogs do, nor do they seem as pleased with the competition. Dogs are natural performers, and they enjoy the shows, but cats are less inclined to have their privacy invaded. Awakened from a good nap to be carried to the ring, they are placed in another cage from which they will be removed for individual judging. They may or may not respond to the judge's handling. They are not as disciplined as dogs, and if they're not in the mood to be frisked and examined, they may dig their claws into their owner or the judge. Band-aids and iodine are a vital part of the scene.

In addition to the recognized pedigreed breeds, many shows have a class for Household Pets, which can be just about anything. They are usually divided into two groups, one of which will be pedigrees without papers, and the other reasonably unidentifiable domestic cats. Even these are beautifully groomed and handsome. Many people travel great distances to show their household pets. The best of these may receive the Morris trophy, or be named King Cat or Queen Kitty.

The shows are long, arduous affairs for the owners and agents, but a lot of fun for the cat lover who has come to look. By the time you have walked up and down the aisles and viewed all the specimens, you will have a good idea as to the kind of cat you want. You can also get the names of breeders who specialize in the breed of cat that turns you on. The cats that are offered for sale at the shows or through the breeders who exhibit there are expensive, but with cats, as with anything else, you get what you pay for. If you want a cat that represents the finest of its breed, you will find it at a show. Any cat is a joy to its owner, but the show offers an ideal framework for comparison.

Shows are sponsored by the cat clubs which are members of a particular studbook association where the pedigrees are registered. There are hundreds of clubs and several studbook associations. A cat may be registered with one or more of the associations, but in order to be judged by any association, he must be registered with it. It is therefore possible to go to a show sponsored by one registry and find a cat that is a champion in another. The main difference between associations in judging standards is acceptance of new breeds and colors.

Psi Trailing

There are many stories of cats with ESP, cats who can tell time (one cat was reportedly able to change over to daylight saving time), cats who can predict an unexpected visitor, or a phone call, but the most lively stories of cat's unusual extrasensory skills relate to those able to find their way home over great distances of unfamiliar territory. This unusual *psi trailing* has been investigated in some depth by Duke University's Parapsychology Laboratory. There are reports of cats traveling as far as 3,000 miles to reunite themselves with their owners after having been given away. Bedraggled and forlorn, they arrive at their ex-owner's door a month or so later, identifiable and relieved. No one exactly understands how they can find the exact house in a strange city, but they apparently clip right along covering as much as thirty miles a day to reach their destination. Beyond the amazing physical and perhaps supernatural feat that this represents, it demonstrates clearly the undeniable loyalty and devotion of a cat to its owner.

All this notwithstanding, our own experience was quite the opposite. When our long-haired male cat was about to reach maturity, just before he had been neutered, he disappeared from our home. He was a beautiful, large black kitten, and we were afraid that someone might have picked him up in a car. We waited three days for his return, then placed an ad in the paper offering a reward for the cat we got for free. We described him accurately as a long-haired, seven-month-old black cat with yellow eyes. The phone began to ring. Someone had found a red-and-black-striped cat they thought might be ours. I thanked them for calling, and said I doubted that he had changed that much in three days. Other calls came from people who had found such diverse animals as a tabby with three kittens, a short-haired, white cat with black feet, and a cat that was mostly black with white stomach and legs. Finally, just as we were about to give up all hope of seeing our kitty again, a call came from a family who said a long-haired black cat had come to the door of their home less than two miles from where we lived. Having heard the remarkable stories about cats who found their way home from California, I was a little dismayed that ours couldn't track the route back for a mile through town.

Nevertheless, we got into the car immediately and went to see the prodigal cat. When we walked in the door, he showed no signs of recognition. We were similarly confused. Apparently in the week or so he had been away, he had lived on the streets and had crossed the threshold of maturity. He had a little kitten voice when he left, but the cat we found had a frightening, throaty growl like a small, underdeveloped lion. His meow had dropped two octaves, and he sounded hoarse. He had also become paranoid. He would not stand in the open. He jumped under a coffee table and behind a chair. He was skittish and frightened. We chalked this up to his experiences on the streets, concluding that he had been fending off a wide assortment of enemies and had learned to take cover fast. Outside of the fact that he didn't act or sound like our little kitty, we decided that it was indeed our favorite pet. My conclusions are that some cats may be more perceptive than others.

Eternally Yours

Whether Cat has actually replaced Dog as Man's Best Friend cannot at this time be irrefutably reported. Surveys and stats vary, as there is an area of unreliability among actual cat owners. According to the Humane Society of the United States in Washington, D.C., a 1988 survey made by N:F.O. Research, Inc., sampling 320,000 households, concluded that there were 56,000,000 pet dogs in America, and between 41.8 million and 57 million pet cats. The gray area in the cat population, the Society tells us, is because the higher figure includes vagrant cats that only show up at the householder's door for feeding, but are not actually part of the household. Dogs are less likely to do this. The lower figure represents cats that live within the house as pets. Dogs were found in 41.3% of the homes surveyed, and cats only in 31%, but the average number of cats in each household owning cats was 2½%. Outside of joint ownership, I don't know anyone who has half a cat, but these statistics indicate that cat owners are more likely to have more than one at a time. In any event, although cats may or may not be the number one pet in America today, the trend shows that the gap is narrowing, and it's just a matter of time before cats will have unquestionably achieved the top slot on the pet parade. As the number of cats owned by American families increases each year, the number of dogs is decreasing. Kitty will soon be King.

The rising popularity of cats in this country is due to several factors. Their personalities, their size and their quiet dispositions make them less troublesome than dogs. As lifestyles change, they are easier to maintain as pets. More people are working outside their homes, and everyone is traveling with greater frequency. Large numbers of cat owners live in apartments or condominiums where a house cat is easier to maintain than a dog that must be walked at regular intervals.

Cats need less grooming, and seem to better know how to take care of themselves. If you leave enough food for your dog in the morning to last him until you get home that night, he will have emptied the bowl by the time you reach the parking lot. A cat, on the other hand, spaces his feedings, eating small amounts of food throughout the day. Your cat may not be waiting at the door with your shredded slippers in his mouth when you get home in the evening, but left with a two-day supply of Kitty Krunch while you go skiing for the weekend, you'll find some still in the bowl when you return.

Cats have also been popularized by literature, movies, and television. While there are only four really famous dogs—Pluto, Snoopy, Sandy and Lassie—the number of familiar cats is endless. People like to read about them and look at them, and never cease to be amused by their antics. They have had a lot of good press. The Cat and the Fiddle, The Cat in the Hat, and Puss 'n Boots are introduced to a baby in infancy. Before the child can read, he or she has learned to love cats. Literature gives us the Cheshire Cat and Mehitabel, while television cartoons feature Tom, Sylvester, Heathcliff, and Top Cat. From the comic strips we have Garfield, Fat Cat, and the first cat star of all, Felix, who, like Garfield, became a popular toy about fifty years ago. Maybe the dogs need a new press agent.

Whatever your cat may be, whether he is the most beautiful cat in the show, or an indisputable variety of a chancy past, he will add a new dimension to your life. As long as he lives, he will be a sympathetic and devoted companion. He will accept the environment that you provide for him, and you will be the most important element in it. His quiet, graceful presence will warm and enhance your home forever. From the lion and the leopard to the Siamese and the tabby, the cat is a creature of eternal enchantment.

Index

About the Author

HELEN POWERS is an award-winning author, playwright, and lecturer, and a former theatre critic and theatrical press representative. Her other books include SIGNS OF SILENCE, a study of Bernard Bragg and the National Theatre of the Deaf, and A PARENT'S GUIDE TO THE 5 U.S. SERVICE ACADEMIES. The author lives in suburban Connecticut with two cats and a poodle.